A Guide to Growing Cassava for Profit

A simple guide for growing cassava profitably

Henry Augustus Roberts, Jr.

Copyright and printing information

Henry Augustus Roberts, Jr.

A Guide to Growing Cassava for Profit

Mr. Henry Augustus Roberts, Jr.,
P.O. Box 150 4000, Buchanan, Liberia,
West Africa
Email: harobertsjr@gmail.com.

ISBN
978-1-83951-0601

Cover Design | Henry Augustus Roberts, Jr.

Table of Contents

TABLE OF CONTENTS CONT'D

Dedication

This book is dedicated to my parents,

H. Augustus Roberts, Sr. and Elizabeth Clarke-Roberts

My mother spent some 42 (forty-two) plus years in the classroom, both as a teacher and an administrator, at several schools in both government and private institutions, in Monrovia and her native Buchanan, Grand Bassa County (Liberia). Her students and the community, fondly, called her "Teacher Aryee" ("T-Aryee" for short). "Mommie", as we called her, had always been and continues to be the inspiration in my life. Her love for us and people in general; her dedication to her work, the church and family; the sacrifices she made for her family; and her prayers, not only for her children's success (especially mine), but for all of the children whom she taught are unsurpassed. Without her prayers and unflinching support, I do not think that I would be alive or would have been able to write this guide.

My father was a lawyer and served in several positions in government including being a prosecutor, as County Attorney (Grand Bassa County) and Assistant Attorney General and finally as a judge, as an Associate Justice of the Honourable Supreme Court of Liberia. But deep down, I think he was actually a farmer. I am not sure whether he considered himself a farmer, but his actions said otherwise. There is no way that what he did with crops and livestock has not in some ways influenced me. At first I had dedicated this book to my mother, but upon reflection, there is no way I could have left daddy out. He raised chickens, ducks, geese, cows, guinea fowls, goats, sheep and hogs; and planted cassava, coconut, grape fruit, oranges, cocoa and rubber. I cannot remember a time when daddy did not have animals in the yard or on the farm. The cows would eat out of his hands and even though, he raised dogs, the geese were more protective of the house than the dogs. I am surprised that he never encouraged me or my siblings to study agriculture. Maybe, for him, it was just a way of life as it is for so many of our farmers.

"May their souls Rest in Peace."

Acknowledgements

WOW! Where do I start from?

There are so many individuals to whom I owe some form of thanks, appreciation and gratitude for being able to be in the position, to produce this guide. Most of all, I must extend thanks and praises to Almighty God, the Most Merciful, the Most Forgiving and the Provider of all knowledge, opportunities and strength. I owe everything to Him who continues to bless me in spite of my imperfections and shortcomings. To Him be the Glory. I hope I have glorified Him in this work.

To the Late Hon. Ruth Caesar, *Developmental Economist, Activist, Advocate, Peace-Maker, and Trailblazer*, who was not only a mentor; but one of my biggest supporters in my agriculture sojourn. When I got discouraged and stopped attending the Ministry of Agriculture's Agriculture Coordination Committee (ACC) meetings, she told me, "Gus, go back to the ACC meetings, don't let those people discourage you. You have a lot to offer and gain by being there." I did go back, and the rest is history. She was my original choice to write the Foreword. What a wonderful and loving human being! I and Liberia, especially the women of Liberia and West Africa, owe Ruth so much. May she Rest in Peace.

To **Ame Atsu-David**, the National Coordinator (2010-2015) of the National Cassava Sector Coordinating Committee (NCSCC) who is one of the main architects of the Cassava Technical Working Group (CTWG) of the ACC; and the inspiration and brain behind the success of the NCSCC. She did not only bring me on the Board of the NCSCC and recommended me to serve as Co-chair, but she insisted that I apply for the CATAS (China) Cassava Production and Processing Technology training for African Countries, even though I did not meet the age requirement. I did apply and was accepted. I can safely say that this guide would not have been possible without Ame's support and the CATAS training.

To the **Peoples Republic of China** for their generosity towards me and over twenty other Africans for a wonderful educational and social experience at CATAS (2013). Not only did we get a phenomenal education in *Cassava Production and Processing Technology*, but we were also afforded a world-class and fantastic hospitality with an opportunity to see and experience China, its culture, peoples, history and cuisine. Much of

African participants at CATAS with instructors.

what I have written in this guide is from what we were taught at CATAS. I am also grateful to the Ministry of Commerce and Industry and Ministry of Agriculture of the Republic of Liberia (particularly, Dr. Moses Zinnah) for approving my selection for the training.

And to Ms. Mercy Lah of the Roots and Tuber Division of CARI for all her assistance and photos highlighting their work.

Special thanks and appreciation to the following individuals who took the time to read, review, edit, and make comments and suggestions to improve the Guide:

1. H.E. Olubanke King-Akerele, former Minister of the Ministry of Foreign Affairs; and the Ministry of Commerce and Industries. "Banke", as she prefers to be called, is a gem. Unlike many Liberians, she encourages and tries to get the best out of you. She has been a major supporter, not only in this project, but in many of other undertakings. May God continue to bless her.
2. The Reverend Sister Mary Lorraine (Retired) of the Catholic Diocese of Liberia and Stella Maris University, who took the time to read the entire guide and provided both comments and grammatical and typos corrections. She spent an hour with me querying me on why I included this and not that. A real teacher, who reminds me so much of mother.
3. Dr, Richardson Okechukwu, a cassava scientist from IITA, author of the Liberia Cassava Feasibility Study (2012). Dr. Richardson, as we call him, was in Liberia for a very short trip (2024), but he took his time to read the draft of the guide and made some very valuable contributions to the final format and content of the book. He also wrote a blurb.
4. Dr. Ophelia Weeks, a neuroscientist and former President of the University of Liberia (UL), for agreeing to read and edit the Draft. Not only did she edit the draft, but she made some suggestions which, I believe, have added value to the guide.
5. To my priest and cousin, the Very Rev. Dr. Herman B. Brown, former President of Cuttington University (Liberia) and Dean of Trinity Cathedral (Episcopal Church of Liberia) for reading the draft manuscript and suggesting some very bold changes and reformatting, which he believed would conformed the content to the intent of the "guide" - its purpose. It was a lot a work, but I think he was very right.
6. My friend and Brother, Hon. Reginald B. Goodridge, Sr., former Minister of Information and Cultural Affairs and publisher of the *Liberian Diaspora Newspaper*, who gave me the opportunity to write in his newspaper expressing my ideas, while developing my writing skills.
7. Dr. Kaysara Khatun of Greenwich University Natural Resource Institute, (England), whom I met quite recently and only had interacted with in ZOOM meetings. In spite of her very busy schedule, she did not hesitate to

agree to my request to review the draft manuscript and provide her professional opinion, which she did.
8. Ms Keren Nekesa, Nairobi, Kenya, my colleague, who also read the manuscript and encouraged me to do a second part.

To my daughter, Denise Elizabeth Augusta Roberts, the apple of my eye and inspiration for what I do. Denise, I thank you for your love and understanding even at this tender age. All you do mean so much to me. This guide is really for you. Being away for school must be tough, but you are always understanding.

To my wife Philomena who has always provided me with much love and support in all I do, I give her not only thanks and appreciation, but much praise for her patience. I am sure that without her support I would not have gotten this far.

Last but not least at all, I would like to express my thanks and appreciation to all the farmers (Cassava, Cocoa, Coffee and Rice farmers), market women, especially the LMA, and farming cooperatives, I have had the pleasure of working with. I would like to acknowledge them not only for the invaluable knowledge they have given me, but also for their patience, willingness to listen to what little knowledge I had to offer them; and for the very hard work and for the many sacrifices they make to put food on our tables with little income or appreciation. They are the backbone and the future of agriculture in Liberia. This guide was done with them in mind. I hope as you embark on your own agricultural sojourn, you will not only consider their work, but you will also remember them and perhaps, include them in your plans.

All the photographs and illustrations in this guide were taken and created by the author respectively, except the following:

1. Page 6, photo of African participants of CATAS. (Taken with author's camera.)
2. Page 11, photo of Cassava beer brewed in Ghana.
3. Page 47, photo of waxed cassava, from Savorysuites.
4. Page 65, photo of traditional cassava planting method using 3 cuttings/stems.
5. Page 71, photo of Ridges created by mechanized ridger (left).
6. Page 71, Ridger-equipped Power Tiller preparing a field.
7. Page 74, photo of laid-out field, courtesy, NCSCC.
8. Page 80, photo of Rubber Mallet, taken from Google Images.
9. Page 95, photos of mechanized Cassava Planters, from Google Images.
10. Page 107, photo of termites, from Google Images.
11. Page 111: photo of Cassava harvester, from Google Images.
12. Page 124: illustration (bottom of page) of Cassava intercropped with corn, created by the author with the assistance of Mr. Kweku of ZEROK using Adobe Photoshop.
13. Page 126: Cassava intercropped with pumpkin. (from CATAS)
14. Page 129, Cassava harvesters: Photo on left from Google Images, Photo on right, from Kwame Nkrumah University of Science and Technology (KNUST), Kumasi, Ghana.

Foreword

Growing cassava has played a vital role in the sustenance and economic stability of communities across the globe. As a resilient and versatile crop, cassava has the potential to provide both sustenance and significant economic opportunities. This guide, "A Guide to Growing Cassava for Profit," written by H. Augustus Roberts, Jr., serves as an invaluable resource for both novice and experienced farmers, illustrating the immense possibilities cassava offers in terms of production, business, and innovation.

Henry Augustus Roberts, Jr., known affectionately as "Henry," offers a comprehensive examination of cassava cultivation from his vast experience and extensive research. This book bridges the gap between tradition and modernity, offering insights into the best practices for growing cassava while highlighting the importance of innovation and technology in agriculture.

Henry's passion for agriculture is rooted in his heritage and inspired by his parents, to whom this book is dedicated. His mother, Elizabeth Clarke-Roberts, known for her dedication to education, instilled in him the value of hard work and perseverance. His father, H. Augustus Roberts, Sr., was a distinguished lawyer and judge with a deep affinity for farming. It is through their guidance and his journey in agriculture that Henry has compiled this guide to assist others in exploring the profitable side of cassava production.

The guide is meticulously organized to cover every aspect of cassava cultivation, from the basics of land acquisition and preparation to the intricacies of crop maintenance and pest control. It also delves into the economic potential of cassava, discussing the global market, value-added products, and the impact of trade policies on the cassava industry. This holistic approach ensures that readers not only learn about the technical aspects of growing cassava but also understand the broader context of its economic significance.

What makes this guide stand out is its practical advice and accessibility. It does not shy away from the technicalities of agriculture but presents them in a way that is understandable to a wide audience. The guide is filled with personal anecdotes and real-world examples, reflecting Henry's commitment to making this a useful resource for all who are interested in cassava farming.

As you turn the pages of this guide, you will find yourself on a journey that goes beyond the fields of cassava. It is a journey that speaks to the power of agriculture to transform lives and uplift communities. This guide is a testament to the enduring spirit of farmers and their crucial role in feeding the world. It is also a reminder that with dedication, knowledge, and a bit of guidance, anyone can succeed in growing cassava for profit.

Whether you're a small-scale farmer looking to expand your horizons or a seasoned agriculturalist seeking new insights, this guide is sure to provide the inspiration and information you need. As you explore its contents, may you find not only the knowledge to cultivate cassava but also the wisdom to embrace the broader impact it can have on your community and the world.

Mariatou Faal Njie
Former FAO Country Representative
Liberia
The Gambia, April 29, 2024

Prologue

After the Liberian civil conflict (1990-2003) and the elections of a new democratic government, there was an influx of both internally and externally displaced Liberians who having sought refuge from the civil war in other parts of the country and from neighboring countries, returned home. The major challenges for the government and international community, at that time, were not only the resettlement of the returnees but providing for their livelihoods and building their capacity to earn some income to be self-sufficient and to, most importantly, rebuild their lives. Naturally, agriculture was the way to go. Cassava being the second staple crop to rice was high on the agenda. The government along with its partners instituted several cassava-related self-help programs in line with its Poverty Reduction Strategy (PRS).

The main challenges of these cassava programs, though done with good intentions, were that they were, in some cases, disorganized and not focused. And in many cases, these interventions were being done in, what could be considered as, "putting out the fire" or just "band aid" approaches. Smallholders farmers were being given Cassava processing equipment and processing centers were being built for them without any consideration for production. Most of these centers, invariably became idled and non-functional. Basically they were just "white elephants".

On May 2012, both the Liberian government and Liberian stakeholders in the Cassava Sector, in collaboration with some donor partners, notably, the International Trade Centre (ITC), and the International Institute for Tropical Agriculture (IITA), with support from the All ACP Commodities Programme (AACP) and financing from the European Commission (EC) developed the Liberian National Cassava Strategy (LNCS). To put it simple, this was an attempt at creating and developing a Liberian cassava industry as enshrined in its vision: *"A dynamic industry contributing significantly to Liberia's economic development, national peace and stability, as well as the improvement of living standards of the Liberian people."*

This vision is clear and in line with the core principles of the Comprehensive Africa Agriculture Development Programme (CAADP), 2003 (Maputo, Mozambique) and later, the Malabo Declaration, 2014, (Malabo, Equatorial Guinea), as envisioned by African leaders, through the African Union (AU) and its agency, the New Partnership African Development (NEPAD). After twelve years of its existence, the LNCS still remains relevant, and it is even more important now with the emergence of the Africa Continental Free Trade Area (AfCFTA).

The overarching objective of this effort was to streamline the numerous and various cassava-related initiatives, and guide the development of the Cassava sector. The LNCS was created along with a board, the National Cassava Sector Coordinating Committee (NCSCC). The NCSCC served as the board, and the board presented the LNCS to the president, H.E. Ellen Johnson-Sirleaf, Liberia's and Africa's first elected female president, and her cabinet in 2015.

The LNCS has the following 6 (six) objectives, *1. Create strong institutions and Coordinate Public-Private Partnership mechanisms for strategy framework development, policy formulation and alignment; 2. Conduct a detail sector analysis to enabled informed decisions on existing empowerment opportunities and incentives; 3. Develop and ensure access to inputs, research and development to ensure adequate development and sustainable production along the value chain; 4. Empower smallholder farmer organizations and foster an entrepreneurship mindset; 5. Improve access to finance along the value chain; and 6. Improve access to technology for production, processing and commercialization in order to achieve quality, quantity as well as consistency.* The strategy was intended to not only bring order to the sector; but to serve as a guide to develop a Liberian cassava industry with the NCSCC guiding the process along with the MOA and the Ministry of Commerce and Industry (MOCI).

Even with the strategy and the NCSCC in place, much did not change. As Cochairman of the board (NCSCC), I had the unique opportunity to work with the then Chairperson, Hon. Josephine Francis and the National Coordinator, Ame Atsu-David (Mrs.) along with other members of the board. With some support from the MOA and the (MOCI), we tried to establish some control, order and develop standards that would be followed by all actors in the sector; and squarely put the NCSCC in charge.

Some of the initiatives of the NCSCC to accomplish these enormous tasks were: *1. The creation of the Cassava Technical Working Group (CTWG) of the Agriculture Coordinating Committee (ACC) of the MOA; 2. Commissioning the Liberia National Cassava Feasibility Study (2012), conducted by IITA under the leadership and supervision of Dr. Richardson Okechukwu; and 3. sponsoring a Cassava scientist, Dr. Joseph Sumo for advance study at IITA.* Another milestone was sending me and a Cassava farmer and processor, Comfort Jallah (Ms.), to the Chinese Academy of Tropical Agriculture Sciences (CATAS) to participate in the *Cassava Production and Processing Technology for African Countries (2012)* sponsored by the Chinese government under the auspices of the Peoples Republic of China Ministry of Commerce, the MOA and the MOCI.

There remains much work to be done to achieve what the GOL and its partners set out to accomplish, as spelled out in the LNCS. I am still of the conviction that this lofty goal of the LNCS is achievable, as I believe, with even stronger conviction, in the achievability of the goals of the CAADP/Malabo (now post-Malabo Agenda: the Kampala Declaration) and the AfCFTA. This guide is my very small contribution to these national, regional and continental efforts, and I sincerely hope that it helps the process.

H. Augustus Roberts, Jr.

Introduction

I know you are very eager to get started, but I believe that before we get into the *nitty-gritty* of this Cassava growing business, we need to get some facts straight- a little bit of history and information on the cassava plant; and some of the business and economic opportunities that the Cassava plant offers to both farmers and would-be entrepreneurs. I think you will agree with me that it was a great exercise after you have gotten the information.

Freshly harvested cassava roots (Yellow Root variety).

Cassava, *Manioc (French), Yucca (Spanish)* is a crop grown widely in most Liberian communities, both urban and rural. In fact, you will see cassava growing everywhere in Liberia and across Africa in general. This makes one, including myself, to believe that cassava plant is native to Africa. However, this might be very far from the truth. Some researchers have traced cassava back to South America, somewhere where modern Brazil is today. Based on this information, I have always believed, and to some degree, I am convinced, that the Cassava plant probably reached Africa via the slave trade aboard Portuguese slave ships. As these Europeans brought their slave ships to Africa to collect their human cargo, they brought Cassava and other crops, that were not native to our part of the world; and they probably, took some of our plant species to the New World (the Americas and the Caribbean) and elsewhere while plying their notorious slave trade.

Cassava growing in someone's backyard in the City, of Buchanan (Liberia).

In fact, the International Institute of Tropical Agriculture (IITA) confirms my suspicions with the following on their website, "*Cassava (Manihot esculenta), is a perennial woody shrub with an edible root, which grows in tropical and subtropical areas of the world. Cassava originated from tropical America and was first introduced into Africa in the Congo basin by the*

Portuguese around 1558."[1] Even with this revelation from IITA, there is another argument which suggests that the Cassava plant's origins are yet unknown and still unsettled. From PNAS (Proceedings of The National Academy of Sciences of the United States) website: "*Cassava (Manihot esculenta) is a staple crop with great economic importance worldwide, yet its evolutionary and geographical origins have remained unresolved and controversial."* [2]

Maybe the cassava plant has its "roots" in Africa after all. But, Honestly, as far as I am concerned, the origins of the plant is not very important. What is important are the economic opportunities it can provide; and its potential health benefits. Both of these important institutions (IITA and PNAS) are very clear on the important benefits of the cassava plant and promote its use, both as food and for industrial purposes, particularly in developing countries.

> **Nutrient content in cassava [3]**
> *The nutritional value of cassava for a dose of 100 grams of tuber contains 160 calories of energy, 0.3 g of fat, thiamine 0.087 mg, riboflavin 0.048 ml, niacin 0.854 mg, vitamin B6 0.088 mg, iron 0.27 mg, and zinc 0 , 34 mg Other nutrients in cassava are as follows: 38.1g carbohydrates, 1.7g sugar, 1.8g food fiber, 1.4g protein, 60g water 27mcg folate 20.6mg vitamin C 16mg calcium 21mg magnesium 27mg phosphorus 271 potassium 14mg sodium.*

Cassava is a very tough and adaptive plant. It can grow in most soils and almost in every climatic condition, even in drought-prone areas. Because of these characteristics, cassava has become potentially, a crop that could help solve some of the food nutrition and insecurity crises in Africa, and perhaps, the world at large; and it could definitely help improve the economic and living standards of smallholder farmers, particularly, women and youth farmers, in sub Sahara Africa. Simply put, cassava has now taken center-stage, and it has, perhaps, become the crop of the 21st century as the demand for Cassava products like High Quality Cassava Flour (HQCF), starch, chips (for animal feed), and other industrial uses continue to grow.

Cassava Leaf being grinded for sale in the market.

Until quite recently, cassava was not considered a major source for nutrients for human consumption, even though, it is widely eaten across Africa; and in many African countries, it is the second staple to rice and maize. This is because cassava is mostly starch and water; and its nutritional information was not readily available. However, some new research have now revealed that cassava does have some nutritional value, and because it is high in carbohydrates, it could be a great energy booster.[4] (See inset above for mineral and vitamin contents.) Additionally, re-

---

[1] https://www.iita.org/cropsnew/cassava/

[2] www.pnas.org/content/96/10/5586

[3,4] https://www.bandingin.com/en/10-health-benefits-you-can-gain-from-cassava

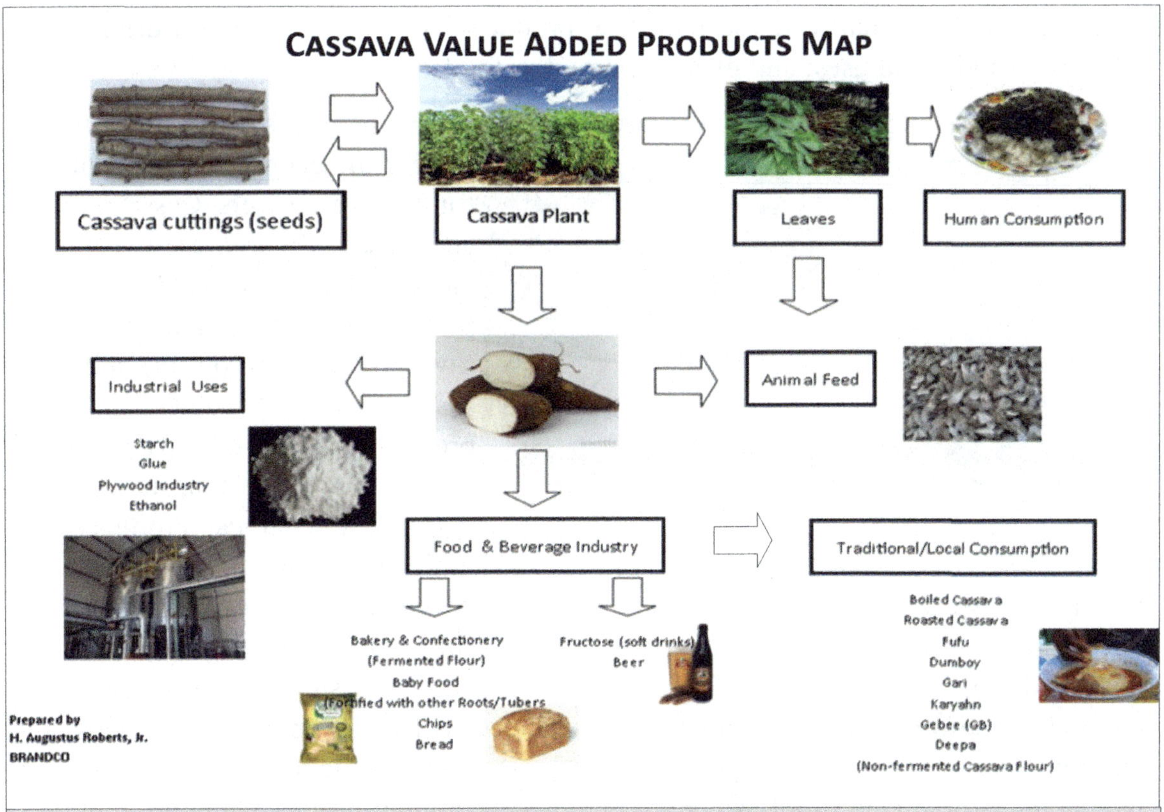

The illustration above is a Cassava Value-added Products Map which was created by the author. It is not a Value Chain Map because the actors and equipment that actually make up and are part of the chain are not included. This map shows the production side of value addition with some of the possible value-added products of cassava, as you can see. A more detailed map would be comprehensive and would include all the actors, equipment and value-added products. You can imagine how vast it is.

searchers, particularly at IITA, in China, and elsewhere are developing newer high-nutrient varieties, like the *Yellow Root* variety which was developed at IITA. The *Yellow Root* cassava is a bio-fortified variety.

Another major advantage of cassava is that it is a plant that has more than a dozen local value-added products (Cassava leaf, Fufu, Gari, Deepa, Dumboy, Gibi, Kanyan, etc.)[5]. Researchers have identified dozens of products that could be processed out of cassava for not only human consumption but also for animal feed and industrial uses. As was earlier said in this publication, the demand for these products continues to grow. As you can see illustrated in the Cassava Value-added products map[6] above, there are a variety of products that can be produced from cassava including High Quality Cassava Flour

[5] Cassava Leaf, Fufu, Gari, Deepa, Dumboy, Gibi, and Kanyan are part of the Liberian local Cassava value-added products. Even though, Cassava leaves are not eaten widely in many African countries like Nigeria, it is widely eaten in Liberia and a major source of nutrients. The Cassava leaf is also the largest-selling cassava value-chain product in Liberia.

[6] This Cassava Products Map was created by the author. A value chain map shows, graphically, a flow of value-added products which could be created from a particular crop, industry or service. It should include the actors, and equipment that make up the chain.

(HQCF), starch, animal feed and industrial products like fructose (for soft drinks) and ethanol for industrial uses; and most importantly, food.

From bread (HQCF) to plywood (Starch), to beer and soft drinks, cassava offers a variety of economic opportunities for cassava growers. Cassava Flour and Cassava Starch are two major value-added products that could provide substantial income for cassava producers (growers) and processors. The demand for these products are continuously growing. For example, Nigeria, and China, two of the largest producers of cassava in the world, have had some serious difficulties meeting their domestic demand for cassava starch and other cassava value added products.[7] Additionally, both Ghana and Nigeria have been using cassava flour in their baking industry for years now; and both of these West African countries, in order to support the development and industrialization of their countries' cassava sector, have even created policies and enacted national laws that compel the use of cassava-wheat flour blend flour for their baking industries. This simply suggests that there are opportunities available right here in Africa, and of course, in China and elsewhere, which our farmers here can profit from.

Fufu as sold in local markets across the country.

In fact, to promote and ensure the use of cassava flour, in January 2005, a new policy, which was enacted by the Federal Government of Nigeria, came into effect, making it compulsory for bakers to use a composite flour of 10% Cassava and 90% wheat for bread production. The government, at that time, projected savings of an estimated US$40 million from the US$400 million it was spending to import wheat to meet its wheat flour demand. The government also projected that this policy would also boost cassava sales, which it did.[8] This simply confirms the opportunities available right here in Africa.

Photo 1: Cassava beer brewed in Ghana.

There are some debates on how effective these policies are, but what is important here, is that these policies, when implemented effectively, not only create economic

[7, 8] *From CGSpace: CGIAR; A Repository of Agricultural Research Output*

opportunities for cassava farmers and processors, but they also help to reduce the use of imported wheat flour and other imported industrial materials which could be easily substituted by cassava value-added products. This, in turn, has the potential of reducing the price of bread, in general, and farmers (especially smallholders), and the other players within the cassava value chain, including consumers, can benefit from these policies. Additionally, these policies also help to create jobs within the agriculture sector, which is one of the major deliverables of the African Union's Comprehensive Africa Agriculture Development Programme (CAADP).

In the beverage industry, Ghana, Nigeria, Malawi, Uganda and Mozambique have been producing cassava beer for several years now, and many soft drinks bottlers are using fructose made from cassava for sweetening. As was said earlier, the number of products in addition to the traditional ones like Cassava Leaf, Fufu, Gari, Dumboy, and Deepa are so many that we could probably write a whole book just on cassava value-added products

In addition to all these opportunities, the *CAADP)/Malabo Declaration* emphasis on Intra-African Trade[9] and the new *African Continental Free Trade Area (AfCFTA)*[10], which promotes free trade and the free movement of goods and peoples across Africa, have, potentially, created an even larger market for cassava and other agriculture products and services in Africa; and as the demand for these products, especially flour and starch, continues to grow, so does economic opportunities for farmers and entrepreneurs within the agribusiness space.

---

[9] *Commitment #5 of the 7 Commitments of CAADP/Malabo Declaration (2014). The AU wants to triple intra-African trade in goods and services by 2025.*

[10] *AfCFTA, established on March 21, 2018, is one of the flagship projects of Agenda 2063: The Africa We Want. The AfCFTA has created the largest free-trade area in the world.*

Purpose of the Guide

In the previous two sections of this guide, quite a considerable amount of time was spent on the cassava value chain and its economic potential - nationally, regionally and globally, especially, with the potential trade amongst African countries with the introduction and implementation of the AfCFTA. As you can see from the presentation, the potential economic benefit to cassava producers, particularly, smallholders (especially women and youth) is tremendous.

Therefore, the purpose of this guide is not to load you up with a lot of unnecessary information or to make you an expert producer of cassava. The intent here, is simply to provide those who are already involved in some aspect of cassava production (and processing) and those who are contemplating getting into the cassava business, a simple guide for the production of cassava; and how one can increase the quantity and quality of their production; and make some money in the process, which should be the ultimate goal. It is also intended to illustrate the new economic opportunities which the cassava plant offers, and why getting into the cassava business, production or processing, would be a good and profitable business once it is done right.

The guide will focus on growing cassava and will discuss all aspects of production: from land selection and preparation, to selecting planting material, to planting, harvesting; and calculating planting material needs, crop yields - both physical and economic.

It will take a very brief look at some of the pests, diseases and viruses that affect the cassava plant, how to identify them, and what steps you can take to prevent and limit the damage they can cause.

The intention here is to make the guide reader-friendly, interesting and useful for everyone, including farmers, the private sector, CSOs, and students. Some aspect of the guide might sound and look technical, but it is not intentional. Agriculture is both science and a way of life; and as much as I might want to make the guide simple for everyone, some aspects of the guide will be more technical than it is intended to be.

The reality is that all aspects of agriculture, including production and processing, are, to a large extent, technical. Because most of our famers are not highly educated, we tend to overlook their work and do not think of it (their work) as technical. The notion is that, *"If they can do it, so can we."* This is a very big mistake. Just think about it. From setting up a nursery to land preparation, selecting planting material, planting, crop maintenance, and management, it takes dedication, patience, knowhow and skills. Farmers might not be able to articulate their work in technical terms and jargons in the way that the so-called educated might be able to do; but their work is highly technical. If you do not think so, try setting up a nursery by yourself without getting someone who really knows what they are doing and how to do it.

Basically, all we (academicians, scientist, researchers, technicians and writers) are doing is taking their skills, knowledge, and the new scientific research results and putting them into writing- a form and language that all of us can read, understand and perhaps, refer to and use not just as a guide but also as a resource, as we build our own farming businesses. I hope the information that I have provided so far and the one in the coming pages will be useful to you as you embark on this agricultural sojourn.

Farming can be fun, very interesting, and it can also be very rewarding. But it is hard work and requires a lot of investments of cash, hard work, patience and time. Your investment will only provide the dividends you desire if you put in the time and are patient with the people you work with.

The Global Cassava Market

As mentioned in the previous section, the cassava value chain is large and comprises many cassava value-added products (starch, flour, chips, ethanol, food for humans and animals, etc.), actors (both large and small), including equipment manufacturers, food processors, bottlers and buyers (consumers) – including the people who actually buy cassava products in bulk for processing; and those who, simply, buy it as food to eat and feed their families and livestock. The value chain also includes the equipment needed to get the job done.

The cassava value chain also includes research institutions like CARI, CATAS and IITA, but also universities and other institutions of higher-learning, whose main functions are to ensure that the best and most productive, diseased-resistant cassava varieties are available to farmers.

In addition to the academic and scientific researchers are market researchers, including, the people and businesses who provide market information services and project the future of the cassava market. In this section, we will take a brief look at what these market researchers are projecting for the future of the global cassava market, what are some of the drivers and who are the players.

Honestly, in the beginning of this project, I really did not plan to get into any detailed segmentation of the global cassava market. The original idea of this project was to present a simple guide for Liberian cassava producers, because I saw many individuals getting into cassava processing, and to some extent, production, with very limited information of the various processes involved and without much consideration or forethought for the market. In fact, most of the people getting into cassava, were mainly focusing on processing. And frankly, this was not limited to Liberian producers.

Unfortunately, many of the donor-supported cassava interventions for smallholders in Africa have, basically, the same focus, processing. "Hindsight being 20/20" and coupled with the evolving nature of a project like this and the cassava industry itself, which is also evolving quite rapidly, it was necessary to adjust the guide to reflect the dynamics of the global food systems (particularly Africa's Food systems) and trade and their effects on Food and Nutrition security.

One example of this is the African Continental Free Trade Area (AfCFTA), which was not a major issue and was just evolving when I started working on this book, some four years ago. However, today, the AfCFTA is rapidly evolving and expected to not only ramp up intra-African trade, but to also increase the free movement of goods, services (including agriculture) and peoples across Africa. At the end of 2023, about five

---

[11] *Free Trade is a policy by which a government does not discriminate against imports or interfere with exports by applying tariffs (to imports) or subsidies (to exports) - Encyclopedia Britannica. The AfCFTA is a Free Trade Area composed of African governments who have agreed to remove traded barriers and allowed the free movement of goods and services and peoples..*

African countries (Benin, Kenya, Rwanda, the Gambia and Seychelles) had lifted visa restrictions in anticipation of the full implementation of AfCFTA; and more are sure to follow in 2024 and beyond.

In respect to trade, the sky is the limit. The AfCFTA has created, by far, the largest free trade[11] area in the world, both in size (55 countries) and population of 1.46 Billion with a combine GDP of US$3 Trillion. According to a World Bank research, *"AfCFTA could lift 50 million people out of extreme poverty by 2035 and expand incomes by US$571 billion. Many of the gains would result from unleashing trade within the continent."*[12] This projection is just with trade within Africa as the research indicates. What then is the projected trade without Africa with the rest of the world?

According to the World Economic Forum (WEF), *"Africa is undergoing profound changes as the region becomes more integrated, accelerated by the AfCFTA - a single market representing 1.7 billion people and $6.7 trillion in consumer and business spending by 2030. The full implementation of the AfCFTA agreement is projected to increase real incomes by 7% or nearly $450 billion."*[13] With these two projections from the WB and WEF, one can really see that with the implementation of AfCFTA, the sky is the limit; and the potential for trading between African states is enormous.

With this new reality, I think a brief look at what is being projected for the future of the global cassava trade is quite appropriate and in place. For this discussion I would like to concentrate the discussions on two cassava value-added products, Cassava Flour and Cassava Starch. However, I believe, that in order to really appreciate the global market potential of the Cassava plant and the opportunities it presents for African trade, there is need to also take a very brief look at the ethanol (bioethanol)[14] market.

The Cassava Flour and Cassava Flour Markets' projections

Before we get into the discussion of the Cassava Flour and Starch markets, we need to ask ourselves couple of questions, "Why focus on the starch and flour markets and not on the others?" and, "What is the difference between Cassava Flour and Cassava Starch?"

Honestly, I think the first question was answered above. The intention was not to get into any detailed market analysis because these issues are mainly related to processing, even though, you cannot process without production, and the discussions in this book are, basically, focused on production.

So, why focus only on the Flour and Starch markets? There are two basic reasons

[12] *Culled from "Africa pursues free trade amid global fragmentation" BOUTHEINA GUERMAZI &MONA HADDAD JULY 26, 2023*

[13] https://www.weforum.org/publications/an-action-plan-to-accelerate-global-business-and-investment-in-africa

[14] Bioethanol is a fuel made from plant material, such as corn or sugarcane. It is produced by fermenting the sugars in the plants with yeast to produce ethanol and carbon dioxide.

why I decided to focus more on starch and flour. The first reason is that, even though, the production of cassava flour and starch have become highly industrialized, they are still the two main products that are traditionally and locally processed by cassava farmers. And even as cassava starch and flour become more industrialized, farmers will continue to produce these cassava value added products for the local market as they have done for hundreds of years before. Why? They are food and provide income.

The second reason is that a detailed cassava market analysis is beyond the scope of this book. Such an analysis could be a book all by itself. The intention here is to just give you an economic reason to get into the business of growing cassava. "Is it worth the time and investment?" This should be the overarching question for you, the investor, to answer.

For the second question, I think that if we are going to explore the Flour and Starch markets, then, it is good to know the differences between the two products. So, what is the difference between cassava flour and cassava starch, especially, when both products come from the same source, cassava roots? As I said above, we are not going into any details here. However, it is important to have the following information.

The differences between cassava Flour and Starch are as follows:

1. Cassava Starch and Cassava Flour are processed differently.
2. Cassava Starch is pure white in colour and is tasteless.
3. Cassava Starch is mainly used for industrial purposes, from food and beverage to pharmaceuticals, to the plywood and textile industries.
4. Cassava Flour is mostly used in food industry as a wheat flour substitute in baking. It is preferred because of its gluten-free properties.
5. Cassava Flour has fibres and some other impurities which makes it a bit darker in colour than Cassava Starch.
6. Cassava Flour is more toxic than Cassava Starch and not meant to be eaten without processing.

As was said earlier, I am not going into too much detail here. If you are interested in processing any of the products, then you need to do a bit more research.

For Cassava Flour, we will look at a report, *"Global Cassava Flour Market: Market Size, Status & Forecast to 2031"* by Verified Market Research[15]. According to this report, *"The Cassava Four Market size was value at **USD 45784 Million** in 2020 and is projected to reach **USD 75958** by 2028, growing at a CAGR[16] of 6.56% from 2021 to 2028."* The report goes on to say that ***"the Global Cassava Flour Market is expected to grow at a very fast pace over the projection period."***

[15] *verifiedmarketresearch.com: "Cassava Flour Size and Forecast."*

[16] *CAGR: Compound Annual Growth Rate or CAGR is the annual growth of your investments over a specific period of time. It is a measure of how much you have earned on your investments every year during a given interval.*

Global Cassava Flour Market: Segmentation Analysis

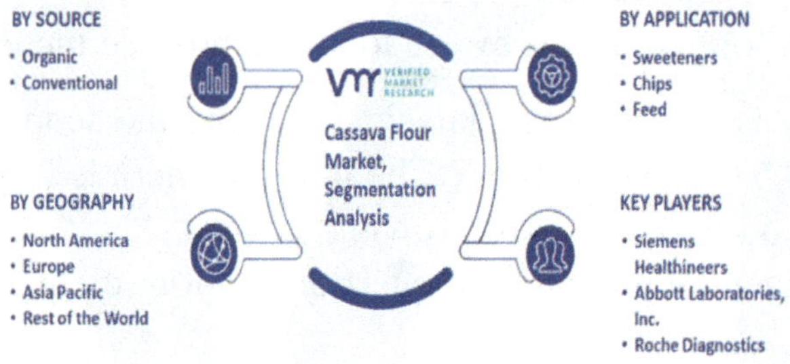

The Global Cassava Flour Market is Segmented on the basis of Source, Application, End Use And Geography.

Cassava Flour Market, By Source

- Organic
- Conventional

Based on Source, the market is segmented into Organic And Conventional

Cassava Flour Market, By Application

- Sweeteners
- Chips
- Feed

Cassava Flour Market, By End Use

- Household Use
- Food Industries
- Bakery and Confectionary

Cassava Flour Market, By Geography

- North America
- Europe
- Asia Pacific
- Rest of the world

Cassava Market Segmentation provided in the Verified report.

The researchers at Verified provide the following reasons for this rapid growth in just the first paragraph of the report. *"The growing consumer preference for living a healthy lifestyle has increased the consumption of healthy food products and food ingredients, which is likely to fuel the expansion of the worldwide Cassava Flour Market. Furthermore, increased per capita consumption of Cassava Flours, rising demand for convenience food, packaging innovation, and an expanding population willing to pay a premium for healthy fruits are some of the factors driving market expansion."* The other reason provided by Verified for the rising demand for Cassava Flour, *"the growing health consciousness, combined with an increase in diabetes incidence, has increased the global demand for artificial sweeteners."*

There is no need to delve into the full detail of the report because it is quite lengthy and available, if you want it. You can get a sample report from the Verified Market's website (https://www.verifiedmarketresearch.com/product/cassava-flour-market)). For a more detailed and comprehensive report you will have to pay for it.

A chart of the Cassava Flour Market Segmentation, provided by Verified, is illustrated above at the top of the page. It provides a Global Cassava Market Segmentation with four components, Source, Application, End User and Geography.

The key players in the Cassava Flour market as listed in the report are: Siemens Healthineers, Abbott Laboratories, Inc., Roche Diagnostics, Bio-Rad Laboratories, Biomérieux SA., Mhogo Foods, Mohan Exports (India) Pvt. Ltd, Dadtco Philafrica B.V., Woodland Foods, Tapioca Vietnam, Vaighai Agro, Psaltry International Limited.

The Cassava Starch market

The global cassava starch market size reached US$ 5.2 Billion in 2023. Looking forward, IMARC Group expects the market to reach US$ 7.8 Billion by 2032, exhibiting a growth rate (CAGR) of 4.8% during 2024-2032. The rapid utilization of cassava starch as an essential ingredient for celiac disease and diabetic diet, increasing demand for natural food additives from the food and beverage industry, and the growing popularity of veganism and vegetarianism among the masses represent some of the key factors driving the market.

For the Cassava Starch market, I am not going to spend much time on it. The information on the Cassava Flour market gives us a good snapshot of the future of the global cassava market. It could be useful as we consider investing in cassava. However, to be balanced, it is good to consider two reports on the Starch market - one from Fortune Business Insights (FBI); and the other from International Market Analysis Research and Consulting Group (IMARC Group).

The IMARC Group Cassava Starch Market Overview[17] is captured in the inset above at the top of the page, and the table below summarizes the information available in the report. A sample of the report can be downloaded from the IMARC Group's website (https://www.imarcgroup.com/cassava-starch-processing-plant). If you want a full version of the report, you will have to purchase it.

Table 1: IMARC Group Cassava Starch Market Forecast

Report Attribute	Key Statistics
Base Year	2023
Forecast Years	2024-2032
Historical Years	2018-2023
Market Size in 2023	US$ 5.2 Billion
Market Forecast in 2032	US$ 7.8 Billion
Market Growth Rate 2024-2032	4.8%

According to the IMARC report, the key drivers of the Cassava Starch market are: *"An Essential Ingredient for Celiac Disease[18] and Diabetic Diet, and The Increasing Demand for Natural Food Additives From The Food and Beverage Industry.*

"Fortune Business Insights (FBI)[19], reports that, "The global cassava starch market Size was valued at USD 40.53 billion in 2018 and is projected to reach USD 66.84 billion by 2026, exhibiting a CAGR of 6.50% during the forecast period." As one can see the forecasts for Cassava Starch from both FBI and the IMARC Group are not very different. Both entities list the same drivers of the market - the textile industry, food and beverages and the health food markets.

17 *Cassava Starch Market Report by End Use (Sweeteners, MSG/Lysine, Food Industries, Paper Industries, Modified Starch, Sago Pearl, Textile, and Others), and Region 2024-2032.*

18 *Celiac disease is a serious autoimmune disease that occurs in genetically predisposed people where the ingestion of gluten leads to damage in the small intestine.*

19 *FBI (Fortune Business Insight's: "The global cassava starch market Size was valued at USD 40.53 billion in 2018 and is projected to reach USD66.84 billion by 2026, exhibiting a CAGR of 6.50% during the forecast period" (https://.fortunebusinessinsights.com/*

Again, I do not think it is necessary to go into the detail of these reports. The key takeaway here is that there is a huge cassava market out there that is wide open waiting to be grabbed. Let us GRAB IT!

THE CASSAVA ETHANOL/BIOETHANOL MARKET

The cassava ethanol market is quite important and should be considered by any country or business that wishes to, seriously, develop a cassava industry. Obviously, any industrialized cassava industry, to be complete and competitive, should consider and include starch and flour production also. This is not to say that the food and animal feed segments are not as important and should not be considered and developed.

In fact, unlike countries in east Asia and China, cassava has always been and remains a major part of the diet of African people, second only to rice and maize, depending on in which part of Africa you live. The only major difference in our part of the world would probably be, how we process and market the cassava-based foods we eat to meet the growing issues of health, food safety, nutrition and mitigate climate and environmental issues.

However, as important as all these cassava markets are, for the purpose of this guide, I think that exploring the cassava Flour, Starch and Ethanol (bioethanol) markets, in detail, should be sufficient in making the additional economic case for investing in Cassava production and processing. The emphasis on production is of particularly importance, because without adequate and sustained production it would be difficult to create a viable cassava processing industry.

Unlike, starch and flour, the production of ethanol (bioethanol) from cassava is more complex and involves several steps and processes; and it needs other necessary ingredients which would make it difficult for the ordinary farmer or processor to produce. Bioethanol production is a more industrialized process. This is the main reason why I was reluctant to discuss the subject. I had concluded that the information on the Starch and Flour markets would be sufficient to make the economic case for cassava production. However, after Dr. Richardson Ochechukwu, a senior Cassava scientist at IITA, and a mentor, read the draft of the Guide, he suggested that I include the ethanol market in addition to the Starch and Flour markets. He was right! And I had to do it.

The Cassava ethanol (bioethanol) market is being projected in the tens of millions of US dollars over the next few years and beyond. According to the experts, ethanol produced from Cassava starch is where the overall ethanol market will see its greatest expansion. The reasons are clear. According to the experts, climate change and the need to produce more environmental-friendly fuels sustainably and cheaper than fossil fuels are the main drivers.

According to an article from the Nigerian Food Journal, *"Ethanol is presently produced from molasses in a number of countries, but cassava, a starch accumulating tu-*

ber crop with up to 30% of fermentable, appears to hold more benefits when used for industrial ethanol production. Firstly, cassava can adapt well to a wide range of growing conditions and requires minimal inputs. Secondly, unlike sugar-based distilleries that are seasonally operated, cassava-based ethanol plants can run year round, due to the crop's rapid growth and ease of harvesting, in addition to its capability to be stored as dried chips." [20]

In addition, when ethanol is produced, there are other by-products, which can be used and sold for other industrial purposes, including dried distillers drains (animal feed production), biogas, which can be used as a supplemental energy resource, and CO_2 (for the beverage industry).[21] This certainly illustrates that the value of the Cassava ethanol market extends beyond just the production of ethanol. It includes the production of beer from Cassava. According to Dr. Richardson Ikechukwu of IITA, a cassava scientist, and lead researcher of the *Liberia Cassava Feasibility Study (2012)*, "Brazil is where sugarcane and cassava ethanol are in large volumes. But countries making beer and alcohol in Africa from cassava are major off takers of cassava ethanol."

In West Africa, Nigeria is, perhaps, the largest producer of ethanol from Cassava with three companies actively producing ethanol from cassava. In addition, in a region were unemployment and internal conflicts, are significantly high and incomes of smallholders are relatively low compared to other parts of the world, increasing the production of cassava-based ethanol and other cassava-related industries makes economic sense. And when you add the AfCFTA and its potential to increase intra-African trade, it becomes even more important that African countries and perhaps, the AU and RECs (ECOWAS, COMESA, SADC, etc.) should start seriously considering PPPs to develop the cassava industrial complex in their regions and across Africa.

**Please note that a list of Regional Economic Communities (RECs) is in Appendix 2.*

It is worth noting, that the internal conflicts, high unemployment, malnutrition, poverty, Food Nutrition Insecurity and the high African food import bill (estimated at US$50 billion) were some of the major reasons why the CAADP and AfCFTA were pursued and adopted by African leaders in the first place. So, I think it makes economic sense, especially as we (Africans) pursue *"Agenda 2063: the Africa we want"*[22] and consider the next steps of the third generation of the CAADP in the various consulta-

[20] Nigerian Food Journal: Enzymatic Production of Ethanol from Cassava Starch Using Two Strains of Saccharomyces cerevisiae Ajibola et al, (NIFOJ Vol. 30 No. 2, pages 114 – 121, 2012)

[21] Cassava Development Authority (CDA), https://cassavaindia.com/products/ethanol/ethanol-process/7th step in, "How to produce Ethanol from Cassava"

[22] *Agenda 2063: "the Africa we want" AGENDA 2063 is Africa's blueprint and master plan for transforming Africa into the global powerhouse of the future. It is the continent's strategic framework that aims to deliver on its goal for inclusive and sustainable development and is a concrete manifestation of the pan-African drive for unity, self-determination, freedom, progress and collective prosperity pursued under Pan-Africanism and African Renaissance. It also celebrates th 100th anniversary of the creation of the OAU in 1963, the precursor of the AU.*

tions being held across Africa with diverse Africans and stakeholders within the agriculture value chain. These deliberations are intended to provide insights that will help inform the design and development of the *Post-Malabo Agenda.*[23] I think that as that our leaders and the designers of the Post-Malabo agenda consider the direction of CAADP for the next ten years (2026-2036); and considering its inherent linkages to the AfCFTA, that we (Africans) start thinking "CASSAVA". Cassava should be one of the major products to consider for industrialization, jobs creation and trade, if we are serious about transforming Africa's economy and the lives of our people.

[23] *Post-Malabo Agenda: is the various deliberations and consultations that were held between the March 2024 and December 2024 to plan and develop the next generation of the CAADP, 2026-2036, the Kampala Declaration.*

Getting Started: Land Acquisition

All agriculture production, whether crops or livestock, has a starting point. Cassava is not any different. So then, where do we start from? If I have guessed right, you might say, "With land selection and acquisition." And you will not be wrong, but not so fast. As was said, this is a step-by-step guide. So, let us go a bit slowly. Yes, you need land, but my first question to you would be, "Why do you want to grow cassava in the first place?" This is a very important question; and it is not just for cassava production. It is a question that you must ask yourself for any agriculture project you are planning to undertake. It will also help you in selecting and acquiring the type of land you need to grow your cassava crop on; and for any other crop you are considering.

In this section we will look at a couple of issues. The first will be based on the question that was asked above: "Why do you want to grow Cassava, in the first place?" The next issue that will be discussed in this section will be, "Where does cassava grow best?" After we discuss and understand these two issues, you will have the information that should guide you in the entire land selection process and not rush into acquiring land that might not benefit you. As was said above, this is very important consideration for any agriculture activity, even processing. The issue related to land conflicts will also be discussed in this section. When added to this discussion, you should be better equipped and informed to go out and get your land and start preparing it for your project.

"Why do you want to grow cassava in the first place?"

Yes! Why do you want to grow cassava? Your answer should be your guide in the entire process, from start to finish. Your answer will also determine how much time, energy and money you will need to put (invest) into the project or business. Regarding cassava, your answer will also help determine what type or variety of cassava you will need to plant.

Oh! So, you did not know that cassava has different varieties? Yes, cassava does have many different varieties. In Liberia, researchers from IITA working along with the National Cassava Sector Coordinating Committee (NCSCC),[24] have identified ten local varieties. The varieties are listed in *Table 2 on page 46.* Quite a few of these varieties were created by Liberian Cassava scientists and researchers at the Central Agriculture Research Institute (CARI) in Suakoko (Bong County, Liberia).

So, you must be clear, very clear, on why you want to grow cassava; and I may add, who you are growing it for? Are you growing it for eating, for processing food, Animal Feed, or for industrial (Beverage, Plywood, Ethanol, etc.) use? Are you growing it

---

[24] *NCSCC: The National Cassava Sector Coordinating Committee was created by the National Cassava Strategy.*

for a buyer in China or is it someone in Ghana, Nigeria or Malawi who needs it to make beer or flour or glue for plywood manufacturing? Or is it for someone right here at home who is just processing Gari or Deepa?[25]

Even if you are just growing cassava in a small backyard garden, just for your family's consumption, you will still need to know which variety to plant, especially, if it is for eating. However, if you are going into this as a *business-for-profit*, then it is very important that you have a pretty good idea of what you are getting into. In fact, another important question would be, "Do you have a market for your product - processed or raw?"

As I was writing this guide, I read an article in a local newspaper (the Daily Observer), where a group had successfully organized farmers to grow cassava. They had grown a lot of cassava but were complaining that they did not have a market (buyers) for the cassava; and they were afraid and very worried that the cassava would rot. So, they were looking to the Ministry of Agriculture (MOA) for help. What could the MOA do or would have done to solve the problem? I am sorry, but I do not think that this is the role of the MOA. The ministry's main role is to implement government's agriculture policies and provide Extension and Advisory services to farmers.

Perhaps, the ministry might be able to help, but what kind of help would they be able to provide? I cannot say. However, I believe that it is dependent on what other services the MOA is offering. Maybe the ministry might have a trade or commercialization section; or there might be a collaboration or sectorial coordination between the MOA and the Ministry of Commerce and Industry (MOCI) to handle issues like these. Maybe one of the MOA's donor-sponsored projects might be able to provide some help, but what kind of help at that particular time of the project? I just cannot say.

However, if I had had the opportunity to speak with the project managers, I would ask them three questions. First question: did they have a business plan? Second question- did they identify a market for the cassava before embarking on such an ambitious project? And the last question: since they are looking to the MOA for solutions, did they inform the MOA about this project before embarking on it? These are very important questions that one should consider before going into any project or business of this nature, especially with agricultural products which have a very short shelf-life.

My advice to this group or anyone who finds himself or herself in this situation would be that they do not panic, because most cassava varieties can stay in the ground for up to three years without really deteriorating except it is one of those varieties, like the *Yellow Root,*[26] that have a specific harvesting time (9 months). This situation the project mangers found themselves in, is one of the major reasons why I decided to write

[25] *Gari and Deepa (non-fermented cassava flour, are two major local value-added products of cassava eaten by Africans.*

[26] *A Bio-fortified cassava variety created by IITA. The Yellow Root is fortified with Vitamin A. It is not Genetically Modified (GMO). It is called "yellow root' because of its yellowish color.*

this guide. So, that a situation like this can be avoided. Yes, they had a good idea, but the best idea without proper planning can become a nightmare with lots of headaches. The most important advice I would offer here would be that before embarking on a project like this, is that you do your homework; and in addition, please consider doing a business plan.

Land Issues

So, having established the reasons why you want to grow cassava, the next issue should be acquiring the land. That is if you do not have the land. As land acquisition is being discussed, it would be good to touch on something that I think is very important- "Land Issues", and the associated problems that could develop from them. If you are not aware of these issues and do not handle them properly, when and if they crop up, you could find yourself bogged down with a lot of unnecessary delays and expenses. It makes no sense to go through all of the hard work and expense of preparing land only to find out that you cannot use it because of some simple issue which you could have handled if you were only aware of it in the first place. In fact if you do not deal with these so-called "simple issues", they can become big and more complicated than you can imagine.

Some of the issues associated with land, include *ownership, land tenure, women's land rights, community land rights, and who has the rights to sell or lease the land?* These are serious issues that are cropping up all over the place and not only in Liberia. If these issues are not understood and handled properly, they can be serious sources of conflicts.

Conflicts arising out of land are serious and can be complicated and expensive to resolve. If you do not acquaint yourself with these land issues and the associated problems that they can pose, you could be in for a major surprise and find yourself involved in unnecessary expenses, headaches and even legal proceedings that could prolong the start of your project or just completely interrupt and possibly end it. Before you know it, someone could be accusing you of "*Land grabbing*".

If you are planning on a large project and intend to purchase or acquire land from the government, an individual, a family or from a community, please make sure that you find and talk to the right people and get a clear understanding of who really owns the land, and who actually has the legal authority to sell or lease it to you. You should do everything legally to acquire the legal rights to operate on the land. Even if you have already bought or leased the land, please double check. Not everyone who claims to be the owners of the land and decision-makers in these communities are who they say they are. Even if you are getting the land from the government, or had gotten it through the government, previously, please do due diligence and make sure that the community decision-makers are or were involved and gave their approval in writing.

If you have to, get the Liberian Land Authority (LLA)[27] and perhaps, a Civil Society Organization (CSO) that deals with land issues involved. Please do so. I would suggest that you get a copy of the new Land Rights Act (LRA)[28] and read it, or have your lawyer explain it to you.

Even if you or your family owns the land and have deed and title to the land, once it is located in a rural community, take all necessary precautions and ensure that you and the community leaders have a cordial relationship; and that they are aware of what you are doing and support you. Land conflicts are real, and there are all kind of unscrupulous individuals claiming to represent the interest of their community, family and the common man, just waiting for the 'kill'. They will not show up until you start developing or have developed the land.

There are families who have developed and run large plantations for years without any problems; but all of sudden, the situation has completely changed. In many cases the problem is not with the community leaders, but some younger members of the community who have no idea or information on how the land was acquired from their parents or the community in the first place. This is not unique to Liberia or limited to large concessions. It is a global issues. A list of some institutions that deal with land issues in Liberia is in the appendix. It is a good idea to know about these institutions because they could help intervene and help resolve conflicts between you and the community when they arise.

Another issue is *land use*. That is having the rights the use the land the way you would like to. Unfortunately, though you own the land and have the rights to use it, the reality that there some limits to how you use the land. Sounds complicate? Yes and No! Yes, you have the right to use the land, but you must use it responsibly, especially if you are going to use it for agriculturally. This is what is referred to as Responsible Agricultural Investment (RAI). So, even though you own the land and should **(profit)** from it, you just cannot use it without considering the needs of others **(people)** and the environment **(planet).** These are the "3 Ps" of RAI. I am not going into a full discussion here on RAI and its 10 principles. Please do the research. However, I will briefly explain the 3 P's.

The 3 Ps stand for: 1. People, 2; the Planet; and 3. Profit. The concept of RAI is that as we engage in agricultural production and processing, we should do it in a very balanced manner. We should first consider the people and their wellbeing, inclusively (culturally, physically and socially). Next we should be concerned about the planet and all the related issues (the environmental, Climate change, sustainability, etc.); and finally we should profit (financially and morally) from our engagement.

---

[27] *LLA (Liberian Land Authority) A government agency created by the LRA to handle all land issues.*

[28] *LRA– Land Rights Act was established in 2018 and passed into law.*

Where does Cassava grow best?

In the case of production, it is very important to know where cassava grows best, especially, when you are at the stage of acquiring and preparing the land for planting.

The following information should help guide you.[29]

1. Generally, cassava should not be grown in areas where it grows best, rather it should be grown in areas where it grows better than other competing crops. This is because cassava just does not compete well with other crops.
2. Tropical and subtropical areas with high rainfall and 4-6 months of dry season provide the best conditions for cassava growing.
3. The soil in the planting area should be thick, loose, and have plenty of potassium (K). This should give high yields with larger tubers (roots).
4. It would be even better if the land area is sandy and loamy. It provides for better aeration, water drainage, and keeps needed nutrients in the soil. This type of soil is good for the cassava plant because it drains water quickly but retains moisture. Cassava does not like a lot of water. Too much water can cause the roots to get rotten (Cassava Root Rot Disease), and we do not want that.
5. Avoid planting on steep (hilly) land as much as possible, it can leads to erosion.
6. If you are going to use a tractor to plough the land try to go about 12-16 inches (30-40 cm) deep or even deeper.

Now I know you must have several questions: "What do you mean when you say, 'Grow Cassava where it grows best,' then at the same time, advise not to grow it where it 'grows best' but rather, grow it where it grows better than competing crops?" That is a very good observation, and it does sound conflicting. But the fact is that the best place (with all the necessary nutrients) to grow cassava might not be where you will get a better result, especially, if there are other competing crops or conditions that might challenge the cassava or inhibit it growth. Rather, it should be grown where it will thrive with less or no competition, The most important takeaway from this is that cassava is not a very good competitor. So, just follow the rule. The information is based on research.

The second set of questions should be, "What do you mean by *"loamy"* and how do I know whether a soil is loamy?" And, "How can I tell if a soil has potassium (K) or any other nutrients?" These are very good questions. So, let us deal with the potassium issue first. Why? Because it is a tricky, and it will, eventually, cost you money. The reason why this is a tricky discussion to get into, is because in the first place, most of

---

[29] *The information are based on recommendations provided by CATAS (Chinese Academy of Tropical Agricultural Sciences) during the Cassava Production and Processing Training for Africa*

us do not even know what potassium is- what it looks like, or how it feels or what it smells like. Secondly, I really do not want to scare you with talk of you spending additional money; and lastly, it can get very technical.

To really find out how much potassium or any nutrient or mineral a soil may have, lack or need, you will have to conduct a soil test. Soil testing is not something that has been readily available in Liberia; Even though, there is a new soil-testing facility here, soil testing can still be expensive. This is the scary part. Somehow, I believe this might not be unique to Liberia; and it is perhaps, just as difficult and expensive in other parts of Africa.

Honestly, soil testing is a must and should be seriously considered if you really want to engage in any serious agriculture production regardless of which crop you want to invest in. Why? Again, the answer is, *"Very Simple- money!"* Before putting a lot of money in a project, you need to have some idea of whether the project will be profitable. In the last two reports of the ECOWAS[30] Regional Joint Sector Review (RJSR),[31] 2020 and 2023, a decline in agriculture productivity across the West African region has been recorded and highlighted prominently. In the various recommendations to remedy the situation, soil-testing is also mentioned and highly recommended.

Please allow me to say this. We need to get rid of this idea that anything can grow in Africa, especially, in Liberia regardless of where or how we plant it? The notion is, *"All you have to do is dig a hole, put a seed in it, cover it, and the seed will grow".* Yes, the chances are that it might surely grow, but what kind of results will you actually get? That is, what kind of yield are you going to get? Secondly, everything cannot grow every and anywhere. In addition to water, sun and air, all plants need certain nutrients, minerals (less or more) and certain conditions to really thrive and be productive.

Lastly, our (Liberia's) soil is not as rich as we think it is. Yes our soil is indeed quite rich, but lots of the minerals in our soil are washed away annually through the process of leaching due to our very high rainfall.[32] So, it is very important to know whether the land you want to invest in can produce what you want to grow in the quantities and quality you will need in order for your project to be a profitable venture. You might need to ask yourself, *"Can Oil Palm grow well here? Or will it be better to plant Cashews, Cocoa or Mangoes?"*

Soil-testing is a serious issue and something to really think about. I believe the MOA is trying to address the situation because it is a must, if we really want to change the

[30] *ECOWAS: Economic Community of West African States is a regional economic body comprising the 15 West African states.*

[31] *Regional Joint Sector Review (RJSR) is conducted every two years by ECOWAS and other RECs to measure the agricultural performance of member states. It is one of the requirements of "Mutual Accountability" of Commitment & of the Malabo commitments. It is done concurrently with Biennial Review (BR), which is conducted every two tears.*

[32] *Liberia has one of the highest rainfalls averaging 200 m yearly.*

agriculture landscape and improve agricultural productivity in Liberia and across the region; and I might add, across the continent. We have not been doing it (soil-testing) here because we did not have the facilities to do the tests; and frankly, it has not really been an issue. Why? Because, all of us believe that our soils are "very rich." In the past, those individuals who wanted to test their soils, had to send soil samples out of the country to be tested. Sending soil samples away to be tested is not only expensive, but it also takes time. However, as was said above, there are some interventions being undertaken to address the situation. There are a couple of facilities available now that can do some of the tests. In addition, IITA has developed a very inexpensive soil testing kit. I first saw it at the IITA facilities in Dar es Salam (Tanzania) in 2023 during African Food System Forum. I am sure the people at IITA might be able to provide more information.

A photo of clay with plant growth. GSA Road, Paynesville, Liberia..

The next set of questions would be, "Where are these new soil-testing facilities located?" How much does it cost? And, "What do I do if the right nutrients and minerals and the quantities required for the crop I want to grow are not present in the soil on my land?'' For the testing facilities, we will list them in the appendix. For the last question, well, this would be, perhaps, the time when we should start thinking of some kind of interventions like fertilizer applications. We will discuss fertilizers later on in the section, *"Fertilizer Use"*.

Now, let us look at the loam issue. What is it, and how can we tell whether a soil is loamy? *Loam* is defined by the Oxford dictionary as *"a fertile soil of clay and sand with humus"*. In Geology, it (loam) is defined as *"a soil with roughly equal proportion of sand, silt and clay"*. I am sure that most of us know what sand and clay are, and what they look like. How about humus and silt?

Humus is described as a dark organic material that forms in soil when plant and animal matter decays. The leaves that drop from trees together with twigs, and other waste material that rot in the soil are what make up humus. Normally, you can find humus under trees where people dump garbage. Sometimes humus develops after trees are felled or in swampy areas with lots of vegetation.

The photo above is an illustration of what clay looks like. See its greyish-colour. It was taken off GSA Road in the city of Paynesville (Liberia) in the wetlands. The photo at the top of the next page (36) is an example of soil with humus and clay. See the

A photo of a field with a combination of Humus, Clay and some silt. See the twigs?

twigs and other decayed plant materials. While this looks like an ideal soil for cassava, I have my doubts. Why? It seems ideal for cassava with all of the necessary elements, but it is located in the lowlands, a swampy area. The first rains would probably flood the field; and that would not be good for the cassava. Because cassava does not like a lot of water. Perhaps if you plant at the onset of the Dry Season, with a well-designed drainage system to drain the excess water from the field, it might work. That is something to think about. But in the meantime just stick with the protocol. If you want to try it, then you will need to plant the cassava in the middle or at the end of October or the beginning of November. But please remember that there is only a 5-6 month window before the rains hit. That could be very disastrous. Remember, it is now raining up to the middle of November and beyond.

Actually, the land above is being prepared for rice production, as usual, by some women for one of the major rice projects in Liberia, Community of Hope Agriculture Project (CHAP).[33] This land could be ideal for a short-term crops like corn and okra, if they are planted at the right time. The moisture in the soil should be able to provide enough water for those crops throughout the Dry Season until they are harvested. Sounds very technical? Well, this is the point I was making at the beginning of the Guide- that some things will sound technical, look technical, and be technical. With agriculture, this is a fact of life. We just cannot avoid it. It is a must that some of these agricultural terms be used, defined, understood and explored. So, do not be shy or reluctant to experiment. You might be very surprised at what new knowledge you might acquire.

[33] *CHAP is a "faith-based "agriculture project that operates in urban areas turning abandoned Wetlands into productive fields. CHAP mostly grow rice, with support from various donor organizations, including the MOA, JACA, SIDA , Concern International and Africa Rice.*

Normally, farmers stick with what they know and are used to. In most cases farmers are not going to try something new that they do not know about or not familiar with. This is not just farmers in Liberia and Africa. This is the nature of farmers all over the world. They will stick to what they know, and what has worked for them for generations. To really get farmers to adopt a new technology or farming method, you have to be patient, encourage and work with them to experiment in smaller plots. This is called Farmers Participatory Research (FPR).[34] In this way the information is just not given to the farmers. They get to see and appreciate the results themselves.

Now, the next question is, "How can we tell whether a soil is loamy?" There is a simple test recommended by MasterClass,[35] a site (www.masterclass.com) on the internet that discusses agriculture and provides some online training to farmers. What is recommended on this site, is that you take a handful of slightly damped (not too wet) soil, squeeze it by making a fist to make a ball out of the soil. Then open your hand and poke the soil with your finger. They say that if the soil is loamy, it will maintain its ball shape when you open your hand. But it will crumble when you poke it. If it does not crumble then it is not loamy.

I am sure most of us might not bother to do this test or even care to go through the trouble; and we will just continue to do what most people do - grow what we want to grow in the soil on the available land we have. However, this is information that I thought you might need. So, it has been provided. Just remember that as much as we want to maintain moisture in the soil; however, for the cassava plant, we also want soil that water can easily drain out of. Cassava does not like a whole lot of water.

[34]FPR (Farmers Participatory Research) is a research methodology that allows farmers to participate in research. This helps to overcome their reluctance to try new planting methods or planting materials. Something we earned as a result of the training at CATAS.

[35] www.masterclass.com

Land Preparation

We have agreed that you need land. So, now that you have acquired the land, you need to get it ready for planting. I also hope that you got it legally with all the rights to do what you want to do with it and on it. Remember, land conflicts and land issues are real.

What are the next steps? You have guessed it. How did you know? The land must be cleared, properly prepared and laid-out for planting. So, obviously you need tools and people who will do the work. Let us leave the labour issue for now and concentrate on the tools. As for tools, you do not need anything spectacular and expensive. The regular stuff (axe, digger, hoe, cutlass (machetes), etc.) will do, if the land is not very large, one hectare (2.5 acres) or less and does not have large trees. Anything above a hectare with large trees, it would be good to start looking at some type of mechanization but nothing large or very expensive.

Now, the question is, "What type of mechanization?" Or, more importantly, what kind of equipment will you need. Most of the time when we talk about mechanization our minds immediately run to tractors, but mechanization is not all about tractors; and there are times when you really just need human power.

Farmers physically preparing land. Lots of work.

A piece of farmland being prepared (under-brushed) before burning. Some of the challenges a farmers has to deal with.

Before I continue on this mechanization issue, let us talk about how land is traditionally prepared for planting. Traditionally, our farmers use the ***slash and burn*** process. That is, they first cut down the trees, then brush and underbrush the land to remove the high bush and grass. After this, they wait for nature to take its course. That is, they allow the cut-bush to dry. After it is completely dried, then they set it on fire and burn the entire farm. After the farm is burned, they remove as much of the burnt fell-trees as possible before actually cultivating and planting.

We have several photos in this section that illustrate the several stages of land preparation. The photo above is a good example of what the land looks like after it is "cut and slashed" before it is burned. The one at the bottom of the page, shows what the land looks like after it has been burnt. As you can see these are some very big challeng-

One of the many challenges farmers are faced with. This is what a land looks like after it is burned.

Mechanization—Land preparation using a tractor.

es for most farmers, even for those who have the money and can afford to pay for the labour or hire the equipment to do the work.

Therefore, you can imagine what the average farmer goes through. Not only does it cost a lot of money, it is time-consuming and labour-intensive. Sometimes it can take up to a month or more just to clear and prepare one hectare for planting. This is why it is important that some kind of mechanization must be considered in land preparation. There is no other way if we really want to be productive and transform agriculture.

As was said earlier, in most cases when we talk about mechanization, the first thing we think about are tractors. But as important as tractors are in agriculture, there are some things they just cannot do. In fact, the tractor might be one of the most important and most valuable piece of equipment a farmer could ever own, especially, if it has all of the necessary attachments and accessories.

The Global Multipurpose Mini Tractor[36] Small, but versatile .

However, the type of mechanized equipment you will need at this time (land preparation), will actually depend on what you are doing and where you are in the land preparation process. If you are cutting down trees, you will probably need a *Power Saw (Chain Saw)* more than a tractor at that time. Because not only do you have to cut down the trees, you also

[36] The Global Multipurpose Mini Tractor is manufactured in Czech Republic by the VARI. Actually, this is an equipment I introduced to Liberia and was trying to introduce to smallholders, especially women farmers. It was successfully marketed in Ghana , Burkina Faso and some other African countries.

need to cut them into smaller pieces *(crosscut)*. If you are at the stage where you need to cultivate (turn the soil over) then you will definitely need a tractor with a cultivator or plough.

If you have the money, another alternative would be to just hire a bulldozer to clear the land. Then you will not need a power saw or tractor at that particular time. However, you will still need a power saw if you are going to cut the felled-trees into smaller pieces (crosscut); and you will now need the tractor to properly till the soil because the dozer will not do it. In fact, with the dozer, most of the roots and stumps would be uprooted and removed. Then you could probably use the smaller, less expensive but effective Power Tiller to till the land.

If you have the money to buy, rent or lease a full-size tractor, it will serve you well, especially, if the land is very large. I must add that even if you have just a hectare or even just an acre, employing the use of some mechanization will not be a bad idea, especially, if you can afford it. It is worth every penny you spend, and it saves time and money (eventually). It is very important that you acquire the right tractor. Not any tractor will do the work you need to do. My recommendations would be that you look at 75 HP 4WD tractors and above if you really want to get the job done.

It must be stressed that land preparation is very important; and how well or bad you do it can affect the final product you harvest. The adage in agriculture is: "What you put in is what you get out"; and this includes land preparation. In fact, some experts suggest that value addition begins at the planting stage; and it includes both land preparation and the quality of seeds you plant and how well you plant them.

Having said all that, it is also very important that while we are preparing the land for planting, it would also be a good idea to start looking for what we are going to plant; and start thinking of how we are going to plant it. It will not serve any good purpose to go through all the expense and labour of land preparation then start looking for planting material, and in the end, you do not find what you need and the quality and quantity you desire. My advice is that you should begin looking for your planting material as you prepare the land or before. We will not spend too much time on land preparation because it is a clear-cut exercise. What we will do is give you some suggestions on how to go about it and provide you with some ideas on what it might cost. I think some of that information has already been provided.

The other advice that I will give here is that if you can afford it, you should de-stump. Yes, you must try your very best to get rid of the stumps and as much of the roots as you possibly can, whether you can afford to hire (rent) a dozer, tractor or not. This will not only give you better results, but it will make life a lot easier and make it much more effective to use a tractor or power-tiller in the future. It will cost you more, but it is worth it. However, there are experts who believe that leaving the roots, and even the stumps, in the field, helps to provide fertilization for the soil as they decay and rot away. But if you intend to use a tractor or a mechanized cassava planter or harvester in the future, it is best to get rid of both the roots and tree stumps.

This is one of the problems which limits the use of mechanization in rice production in Liberia. If we really want to improve rice production in Liberia and meet our consumption requirements, we need to employ the use of mechanized equipment, especially the use of the *Combine Harvester*, sometimes referred to as the "combine", at harvest. The combine harvests and threshes the rice, all at the same time. This is just putting it in simple terms that most of us can understand. But technically, the *combine* performs four harvesting processes - reaping, threshing, gathering, and winnowing in a single process. The combine is not only used with rice, it is also used in harvesting other grains (Corn, Wheat, Soybean, oats, etc.). But it will not work effectively the way it should, if the rice or corn field is littered with tree stumps and roots as most of our farms are planted.

This is picture of a Combine Harvester in operation taken by the author while on a agro-mechanization training program in India (2013).

There are mechanical cassava harvesters available also, but they do not work like the combine harvesters. Maybe one day we will get there. We will discuss this later. Even though, we are discussing cassava, I thought that providing the information on the combine harvester would be a good thing because most of our cassava farmers are also rice farmers.

What really prompted me to discuss the combine was an experience I had at a rice-harvesting ceremony I participated in while editing the guide. At these harvesting ceremonies hosted by a community self-help project funded by some international donors, there was a bumper crop, but the rice was being harvested manually. An official from Africa Rice[37] realizing the inefficiency and high losses occurring commented that there was a need for a mechanized harvester because he believed that much of the harvest would being lost in this process.

[37] *Africa Rice is formerly WARDA (West African Rice Development Agency) which was headquartered in Liberia at CARI. It is now headquartered in the Ivory Coast.*

Characteristics of Cassava

In addition to the several different varieties, there are several characteristics of cassava that one must and should be aware of before going into the business of cassava production or processing, including where it grows best. In this section, we will look at some of the basic characteristics of cassava: its perishability, its make up, including the substances it produces. We will take a look at some of the more important characteristics of Cassava that are related to production.

Cassava and Cyanide

An important issue/characteristic of cassava that you should be aware of is that the cassava plant produces cyanide.[39] Honestly, it is not as simple as that, but we really do not want to go into any in-depth science here. That is not the objective of the guide. The main thing to know here is that cyanide can be harmful to your health. It is poisonous, and it is in cassava (actually produced by cassava). It only becomes a problem if the cassava or its leaves (for those of us who eat the leaves) are not handled or processed properly.

Please, do not panic. The amount of cyanide in cassava (or that it produces) varies from variety to variety, and most of it dissipates when the cassava or its by-product is processed properly. But you must know that the stuff is there. So, now it must be obvious, that if you want to grow cassava for eating (human consumption) you must select a variety with less cyanide content because, as was said above, cyanide is poisonous. Based on the aforementioned, it can be concluded that not all types of cassava are good for human consumption, especially, when eaten raw. Even low levels of cyanide can be dangerous when consumed over a long period; and it has been linked to goitre. But as was said earlier, there is no need to panic.

Our people have been growing, processing and eating cassava for centuries, and they have good knowledge about it; and with new scientific research the problem is basically not a big deal because we know which variety has less or more of the substance (cyanogen) that produces cyanide and how to deal with it. How can we tell which variety has more or less cyanide? There is a simple taste test. The sweeter the cassava tastes, the less cyanide it has. The more bitter it tastes, the more it has. Please do not make it a habit of eating raw cassava because it tastes sweet. In the long run it could be bad for your health. I know that some people, especially those who have been eating raw cassava might argue about this, nevertheless, it is important for you to know that there is an associated risk with eating raw cassava. Quite recently, at an international workshop, a colleague argued and disagreed with me on my recommendation of not eating raw cassava. Obviously, he has been eating raw cassava all his life and nothing

---

[38] *This is not only a characteristic, it is also an issue, a potential health issue.*

has happened to him. But I stand by this.

Now, let me be honest, real honest with you and tell you why I have provided this information. In 2015, as a member and Co-Chair of the NCSCC, I had the privilege of attending a Cabinet meeting where the committee presented the Liberia National Cassava Strategy (May 2012)[39] to the President (H.E. Ellen Johnson-Sirleaf)[40] of Liberia and her cabinet. After presenting the strategy, the first person to raise their hand to ask a question was the Minister of Health. What do you think was the Minister's issue? "Cyanide" and its health consequences. Fortunately, we were able to respond adequately to the Minister's concerns. I want you to be in the position to respond adequately also when the issue comes up.

We are aware that there was some work at Ohio State University (USA) where in 2003 two researchers (Richard Sayre and Dimuth Siritunga) successfully created *cyanogen (or cyanide)*-free cassava plants. Their work is on-going, and it is hoped that someday soon we might not have to be concerned about the level of cyanide in cassava. Until then, it is important that you have the information and take the necessary precaution, because the potential for health problems is there. That is why we advise that people avoid eating raw cassava excessively. As was said above, it is not a good practice. Eating raw cassava over a long period can pose serious health problems just as the Minister of Health pointed out and was concerned about.

Table 2:
Ten local cassava varieties identified by IITA in the Liberia National Cassava Feasibility Study with their estimated harvesttime, average yields, and uses .

No	Variety	Harvest (Months)	Avg Yield Mt/ha	Use
1	Bassa Girl	3-9	3.4	Table (Boil & Eat) Cassava, Fufu, Dumboy
2	Maatadi	3-24	3.3	Table (Boil & Eat) Cassava, Fufu, Dumboy
3	Butter Cassava	3-9	3.9	Table (Boil & Eat) Cassava, Fufu, Dumboy
4	Cariecass (2 & 3)	6-12	3.1	Table (Boil & Eat) Cassava, Fufu, Dumboy
5	World Bank	3-12	3.8	Table (Boil & Eat) Cassava, Fufu, Dumboy
6	Gbofani	9-12	3.6	Industrial: Fufu & Gari
7	Calabar	3-6	3.7	Table (Boil & Eat) Cassava, Fufu, Dumboy
8	Coco	3-6	3.4	Table (Boil & Eat) Cassava, Fufu, Dumboy
9	Red Leaf	3-9	1.9	Table (Boil & Eat) Cassava, Fufu, Dumboy
10	Ivorian	3-6	n/a	Table (Boil & Eat) Cassava, Fufu, Dumboy

39 *The National Cassava Strategy (May 2012) was a five-year strategy developed by the government of Liberia and some of its donor partners to create a vibrant and sustainable cassava industry in Liberia. The National Cassava Sector Coordinating Committee (NCSCC) is a by product of the strategy.*

40 *Mrs. Ellen Johnson-Sirleaf was the first female elected President of Liberia and in Africa. She was elected for 2 (two) terms and served for 12 years (2005-2017). It was under her administration that the National Cassava Strategy was developed.*

Cassava is very perishable

Another characteristic or I would say, "bad side of cassava", that one must be aware of, is cassava's perishability. Simply put, Cassava is very perishable. This is very important information to have, if one is growing cassava for commercial purposes, especially, if you intend to export raw tubers (the cassava roots).

Basically, after 24 hours, cassava begins to perish. At about 48-72 hours, it is basically useless for processing except in very few cases. This is true for many other plants, crops, fruits and flowers. So, it is important that one does everything possible to start processing cassava within 24 hours after harvest to get the best out of it.

One of the major challenges cassava producers and researchers are faced with is how to preserve cassava. We are not going into too much detail here because some of the methods of preservation can be very expensive. I would not be too concerned about this except you are planning to export raw tubers. In that case, you will really have to do the research and find the best and least expensive solution. However, if you must know, the two major ways of preserving raw tubers are to either use wax or freeze-dry it. Most of the cassava roots exported to the USA and Europe are either freeze-dried or waxed. The tubers bought in supermarkets and convenient stores in the US and Europe are mostly waxed tubers. Both processes can be relatively expensive. However, because of the high African and Caribbean population in the US, Canada and Europe, this could be a very lucrative market for cassava producers.

Waxed Cassava

These cassava roots have been waxed. See how shining they look. That is from the wax covering the cassava tubers/roots. (Photo, courtesy Savorysuites)

If you are really interested in cassava preservation or intend to ship raw tubers, you can go on the websites of Savory Suitcase: IITA and Postharvest.[41] This website offers excellent information on extending the life of cassava roots.

As was said earlier, preservation is a major challenge for all agriculture products. If you are processing you must start the process within a specific time period relative to the shelf-life and processing requirements of the particular produce. The closer you are to this timeline, the better processed-product you will have. For example, to get good quality processed Palm Oil, you have to process the palm fruit within 24 (twenty-four) hours after harvest. This is why the major Palm Oil processing facilities want their out-growers and suppliers of the palm fruits to be within 40 kilometres (about 24 miles) of their factories. The same principle and practice can and should be

[41] www.savorysuitcase.com; (https://propas.iita.org/en/solution; postharvest.biz:https://www.postharvest.biz/en/

applied to the cassava value addition process.

Why is this so important? Not only does this affect the quality of the product you are trying to process from the raw material you are producing, it also affects the price you finally you receive for what you are going to produce. And inherently, it affects your business and the economy of the country. Getting your produce to the market in a timely manner is very important. Unfortunately, in many cases there are many factors (poor infrastructure, limited transportation systems, inadequate extension services, poor roads, etc.) which farmers and agribusinesses have no control over that delays and sometimes prevent their produce from getting to the market on time. These are some of the reasons for the high post-harvest losses (PHL) in our part of the world. But this is a different topic for another time. So, the advice is that you to do your very best to control those things which you are capable of handling. And leave the rest to the government's imaginations.

Cassava Varieties

As was indicated earlier, there are different varieties of cassava, and I have mentioned some of the varieties that are available in Liberia. There are other varieties which were created by IITA, and they are also available here. An updated list of cassava varieties from CARI is on page 147 (Appendix 4). This is very important information to have because, it is very important that you acquire the right variety for your project. As was highlighted earlier, that the variety you select should be based on the particular value-added product you or your customer want to process. Your production must be guided even if it is just for your personal consumption.

This was discussed earlier, so, I really do not want to repeat it here. But it is very important that you understand that your final product should determine the variety you select to plant. If you want to supply someone or an entity that is processing a cassava value-added product for a school-feeding program, then you might want to produce the Vitamin A-rich Yellow Root variety. If it is for industrial purposes you, must select the variety that will provide the substance you want and the quantity that will make your venture profitable. For example, if you intend to produce starch, you will need a cassava variety that will produce cassava roots with high starch content. If you are processing for food, you need one with the least amount of cyanide, what is called the "table variety". I think you got the idea.

So, now that you have some basic information and know exactly why you want to grow cassava, which variety you will need to plant; and you have acquired and prepared the land. Now it is time to get down to business.

However, before we go on, I am sure that you are asking yourself, "But how can I find out which variety I need to plant to meet my needs?" Good question! The experts are available. The best place to go is to your national agriculture research institute. For us in Liberia, it would be CARI. In Kenya, it is Kenya Agriculture Research Institute (KARI). In Sierra Leone, it is Sierra Leone Agriculture Research Institute (SLARI). This is just to name a few of these national research institutes. Perhaps, in your country there are private research institutions in addition to the national institute. They might also be able to help you.

IITA is, perhaps, the best place go. For West Africa, IITA is located in Nigeria (Ibadan); and most of the information they have is shared with the national research institutions of each member country, not with individuals. So, your national research institute might just be the best place to go anyway. They should have the information from IITA. For us in Liberia, in addition to CARI, the NCSCC should also be a place to check as per its mandate. If they do not have the information, they might be able to direct you to someone who might have it. But again, I am sure they will redirect you to CARI. Quite recently (October 2023), I was in Tanzania and had a very enriching experience at the IITA facilities at Dar es Salam. They are doing some very wonderful work in Tanzania.

Do not be too concerned about this. The information is available. At this stage, we just want to make sure that you are aware and understand that cassava varieties must be considered in production and processing. Later, when we get to the point of actually selecting the planting material of the variety you will need to plant, we will look at some of the ways in which you can identify different varieties, especially local varieties. For now, we just want you to know that your project (what you want to grow or process) and your intended market will determine which variety you will need to grow. In the table on page 46 ten local cassava varieties identified by IITA in the Liberia Cassava Feasibility Study are listed with their various uses. As was said earlier, there is an updated list from CARI which is available in the appendix.

The photo on the previous page is a cassava variety I saw quite recently (August 2024) while I was taking my morning walk as I was editing the guide for publishing. Honestly, I have not seen this variety and unfortunately, the old lady selling the cassava did not know the name of the variety and neither did I. All she said was that it was "Sweet Cassava". The photo above is, basically, a Cassava tree. It is another one of the photos I took while doing my routine morning walk. Sometimes you see these cassava trees that do not grow as cassava would normally grow or what you will see in a cassava farm. Interestingly, they are never harvested. They just grow as an ordinary tree. The various photos of the cassava plants in this guide illustrate the nature and complexities of the Cassava plant.

Planting Materials

As was stressed earlier, you should start looking for and getting your planting materials as you start to prepare the land or even before. That is if you are serious about your project. Do not worry, they will not spoil (for a lack of a better word), if you store them properly. So, hopefully the land is being prepared, and you are now looking for the planting materials. I would suggest that you get someone or an institution that knows about this to help you. Why? Very Simple! Most of us, including the so-called experts, like myself, have a difficult time identifying the various cassava varieties. So, it is good to get someone who knows what he or she is doing. Remember, earlier I did talk about the different cassava varieties, but at that time, I was, simply, presenting the information that there are many varieties of cassava, what they are called, and what they are used for in the cassava value chain. Now, we are talking about acquiring the actual physical planting material, the real stuff. Table 2 at the bottom of page 46 lists some Liberian varieties (planting materials) with their harvesting times, estimated yields and uses. The updated list in the appendix 4 (pages 147-148) provides a bit more information than the table 2.

What we do not want and must do all we can to avoid, is to have two or more different varieties planted together in the same field. This is why it is very important that you make sure that you get what you need and want for what cassava value-added product you want to produce. This is very critical. Do not just go out and start buying cuttings without stressing the variety you want for what you want to process. For example, if you are looking for a variety that is good for Gari production and find two or more varieties that will produce what you want, try your best to select one and plant that one. Or get both, but plant them separately. In this way you will get to know which one is better for your intended purpose.

In the case where you find two varieties that are good for Gari production you can acquire both if one of the varieties will not be enough for your project, But do not plant them together in the same field (plot) or in close proximity of each other. You can plant multiple varieties, but they must be separated and not planted in the same plot. In other words, you could plant one area or plot with *Bassa Girl* and another with *World Bank*, but they must be separated by a corridor of at least three to five meters (about 9 to 15 feet).

Let me say this once more, with emphasis: ***"Under no circumstances should you plant two or more different cassava varieties together in the same field (plot) or in close proximity to each other. It is even worse if you were to mix, for example, Gbofani, a variety mainly used for Gari/Farina, with a table variety like Bassa Girl or the Yellow Root."*** I have seen cassava farms with up to three different varieties planted together. You might not think it is a problem, but just wait for harvest. That is when you will start having problems. How would you differentiate one variety from the other variety in your field?

Do not do it and do not allow anyone to convince you that it is okay to do so. You know how it goes: *"We do it all the time. It will not do any harm."* It does something, and it could cost you a whole lot of money and lots of headaches. **DO NOT DO IT!**

Now, I know you are asking yourself, "Why shouldn't I." This is a good question, but one you could answer yourself, if you really think about it. Cassava is not the only plant that has different varieties, So does okra and corn, just to name a couple. There is sweet corn and not so sweet corn. Would you want to plant sweet corn and a another variety together in the same field? I do not think so! You would have a very tough time separating the two different varieties of corn at harvest.

The same thing would apply to Okra, if you were to plant the six-week variety with a longer-term one, or lady fingers with one of the spineless varieties like Clemson Spineless [42] or with one of the reddish varieties. And so it is with cassava. Imagine planting a table variety, like Bassa Girl[43], with an industrial variety like, the 419[44] or Gbofani.[45]

How about the Yellow Root with Cariecass? Not only would you have a difficult time at harvest separating the production, but eventually, if you keep mixing varieties you could end up with a new variety unintentionally. There is something called cross pollination, remember? These are some of the reasons why one should avoid placing different or multiple crop varieties in the same field. You can imagine how disastrous it would be with rice? So, again, do your very best not to plant multiple varieties of crops in the same field, not only cassava.

I would suggest that if you need confirmation on this, a good place to go would be the experts at CARI and the MOA, for Liberians; or the national research institute where you are located. They can be of real help. Or, you can contact me. But remember what I said earlier, that even the experts, like myself, do have some difficulties identifying the various varieties. However, we (the so-called experts) can still ensure that you get the right information by directing to the people who can help you, if we cannot provide the information ourselves.

The NCSCC, with the assistance of IITA, has identified ten local varieties. Most of these varieties were created by our own (Liberian) cassava scientists at CARI. These are listed in both *Table2* on page (46) and the updated list on page 147 and 148. However, there are other local cassava varieties which are not listed in either of the tables. These other local varieties have been given names by the farmers in their particular locality. Usually these names are given based on production characteristic of the cassa-

[42] Clemson Spineless: An Okra variety.

[43] "Bassa Girl" is a local table Cassava variety grown widely in Grand Bassa County, Liberia.

[44] The 419 is TME 419 variety, one of several high-yielding diseased-tolerant cassava varieties developed at IITA. Others are TMS 30572 and TMS 98-051. For more information on these varieties, contact CARI or IITA.

[45] Gbofani is another local Liberian Cassava variety. It is mostly used for Gari production.

va. For example in the Owensgrove District of Grand Bassa County (Liberia), farmers have introduced me to two varieties not officially identified or listed by IITA or CARI, *Nyahnegbloh* and *Ben Urey*.

The first one name, literally means, *"Bring your bag"* in the local language (Bassa) of that area of the country, Grand Bassa County. The name suggests that the variety produces so much that at harvest, all you need to do is to bring your bags and load up. The second one is named after one of our local entrepreneurs, a farmer himself. I asked them why they named this variety after the gentleman? They said, *"It is 'rich' like him."* This simply means that this variety is very productive. This is being highlighted because in your search for cassava cuttings, you might come across these varieties and wonder why they were not listed or identified by CARI.

Interestingly, quite recently, as I was editing this book, I visited the main market in Lower Buchanan, Grand Bassa County (Liberia), my hometown to look at some of the cassava that was being sold. I was introduced to two other varieties which I had never heard of. One was called Dyuwé (yu-weh), which means "Elephant" in the local language, Bassa. Obviously, you can guess why they call it "elephant". The other, which name I cannot really spell, means, "Go tell the news to the town." In other words, the harvest is plentiful, so, take the news to the town.

In fact, I believe that these varieties might actually be some older cassava varieties that were probably created or distributed by CARI or the MOA, but the farmers just do not know this. Remember, we had a long civil conflict, and many of our people were displaced, had to leave their communities and they fled to other areas in the country seeking safety and refuge from the war. Because people were moving from place to place and community to community, they probably took some of these varieties, not knowing what they were called or which variety they were, along with them and planted them where they ended up. Remember that most of our people (about 75%) are farmers. So, they planted what they had and named them accordingly.

Additionally, after the Liberian civil war, the United Nations (UN) and many relief agencies provided some of these cassava cuttings to farmers to help them restart their lives. They, perhaps, provided what was available without any knowledge of where they came from or which variety they were giving out to farmers. One example is the *World Bank* variety. Did the World Bank develop a particular cassava variety? I do not think so. At least, I am not aware of this. This was probably a variety distributed to farmers by some World Bank project. As far as the farmers were concerned, these were from the World Bank. So, they called it *World Bank*, and the name just stuck.

On a closer look at the *World Bank* variety, you will see that it has a lot of similarities to one of the Cariecass varieties created at CARI; and therefore, it just could be a derivative of the Cariecass or actually Cariecass. But when the IITA researchers asked the farmers to identify the cassava variety, that is what they called it, *World Bank*, and they still do. The same thing applies to many of the other varieties.

I am also of the opinion that some of the varieties are the result of planting multiple varieties in the same fields. Cassava, like other plants, produces seeds. It is very possible, from my perspective and training, that as a result of cross-pollination, newer varieties could have developed right in the field under an uncontrolled environment. This conclusion is derived directly from the training I received in China at CATAS. Each student of the class was required to do a cross-pollination activity.

Since the end of the civil war some twenty years ago, things have returned to some degree of normalcy. The Central Agriculture Research Institute (CARI), in the last ten years or so, have been collaborating with IITA, and together they have introduced several dozens of *"improved varieties"* which are propagated by CARI and then released and distributed to farmers. It is very important that you understand what we mean by "improved varieties". Most of our local varieties are diseased; and hence, they are low-yielding. The improved varieties are disease-resistant and high-yielding. We mentioned the Yellow Root cassava earlier. It is one of those "improved disease-free varieties". It is also a bio-fortified variety. It is not a genetically modified (GMO) variety. We have to be clear on this. Why? Because there is lot of controversy around GMOs and therefore, it is important that this clarity is made. There is a difference between GMOs and bio-fortified crops. No! I am not going into any details on this subject. If you need additional clarity, please do the research. But the two processes, Bio fortification and Genetic modification are very different.

There are other bio-fortified crops besides the Yellow Root cassava. The Orange-flesh Sweet potato is also bio-fortified and there are bio-fortified beans also. There is a concerted effort being made by the AU to encourage the consumption of these bio-fortified foods because they provide much of the nutrients, protein and vitamins that are missing from our diets. Why? The malnutrition rate in Africa is very high, and the AUC, is very concerned about this. Commitment 3 (Ending Hunger in Africa by 2025) of the CAADP Malabo Declaration tries to address this by setting nutritional targets to reduce the incidence of stunting, wasting and obesity, which are alarmingly high amongst African children under five years old.

The AU's Department of Agriculture Rural Development, Blue Economy and Sustainable Development (DARBE), in an effort to reduce these high malnutrition rates, is not only promoting the consumption of bio-fortified foods, but it is also measuring and tracking how member states are performing in ensuring that these bio-fortified foods are reaching the most vulnerable segment of the African population - children under 5, pregnant women and lactating mothers. A new performance category (PC) to measure this has been incorporated into the CAADP Biennial Review. This is an assurance that consuming bio-fortified crops, like the Yellow Root is not only safe and good for you and your children, but it is also good business to invest in their production.

Identifying Cassava varieties
(How to tell the difference between Cassava varieties?)

Now I guess you might still be saying to yourself, "Yes, this is all good, but how can I tell the difference between the various cassava varieties? What is the difference between *Bassa Girl* and *the Cariecass varieties,* or *World Bank* and *Gbofani*?" These are very good questions, especially, after I have admitted that, even I have difficulties identifying the various cassava varieties. Maybe, I should be able to, but one thing I have learned in life is to be honest. If this is something that you are not doing everyday, then you will have some difficulty, and I will admit that I do have difficulties identifying the various varieties.

And, quite frankly, the more you get into this cassava business, the more varieties you will come across which you just might not be able to identify as I experienced quite recently. But we do have the experts, normally cassava farmers, themselves, who are quite capable of telling the differences between local cassava varieties. Cariecass 1, 2 & 3 are listed in both *Table 2* on page 46 and the updated list from CARI (page 147 & 148). So, how does one tell the difference between *Cariecass 2* and *Cariecass 3*?

What about the newer high-yielding varieties like the Yellow Root and 419 varieties from IITA? Yes, there is a 419 ("Four-One-Nine") variety created at IITA in Nigeria, (Ibadan). Would our farmers be able to identify them in the field? For these varieties, you will just have to rely on CARI and its certified out-growers. Eventually, farmers, and hopefully, all of us, will also be able to identify these newer varieties. It takes time and constant use.

Cassava varieties can be identified by the following ways:

- The size and shape of their leaves.
- The colour of the stems
- The colour of the leaves.
- The colour and shade of the bark/stem.
- The growth pattern– e.g., Cariecass II develops two branches as it grows, while Cariecass III develops three branches.
- Root size and colour
- The colour of the flesh of the tubers, e.g., *Yellow Root* variety is yellowish. The colour of most cassava flesh is white.

Let us take a careful look of the group of photos on the next two pages (56 & 57). Let us first take a look at the inset on page 56. Can you see the physical differences of the several cassava varieties pictured? Would you have been able to tell the differences if they were not pointed out in the text below the photos?

Next, let us look at the several photos on page 57. Again, take a look at the photos and see if you can identify the physical differences, colour, size, and height of the cassava

The differences between Cassava varieties.

In the photos above we have five cassava plants. Even without naming which variety they are, we can see physical differences and different growth patterns. Let us look at them in detail in the photos, clockwise (L-R) beginning with #1. In #1, see the arrows pointing to the stem. The stems are red. In #2, what color are the stems? They are light green. In #3, look at the points of the arrows. This plant has three branches. In #4, look keenly at the cassava plant in my hand and the one on the grown. The one in my hand has red stems but look at the leaves. They are quite different from the Red-Stem one in #1. The leaves are not only narrower, but they have a purplish color. The one on the ground (Arrow) the leaves are very different from all of the other plants. It is obvious from these photos that these are five distinct cassavas. varieties. An even closer look at Photo #4 tells us that there are two different varieties growing in the same field. How can you tell? Take another very close look at the leaves. Do you see any differences between the cassava in the foreground? What does this tell you? There are two different varieties being grown in the same field. We should try to avoid this.

Physical Differences in cassava varieties

In the photos above you can observe some physical differences of the cassava plant. In photo #1, the cassava sticks have dfferent colors. This is a clear indication that these are different cassava varieties. In Photos #2 & #3, there are two cassava plants growing. The one in Photo #2 is shorter than the one in Photo #3 and the steps are red. These are physical difference that you can easily see. Which cassava plant do you think you will get more cuttings from per stick?

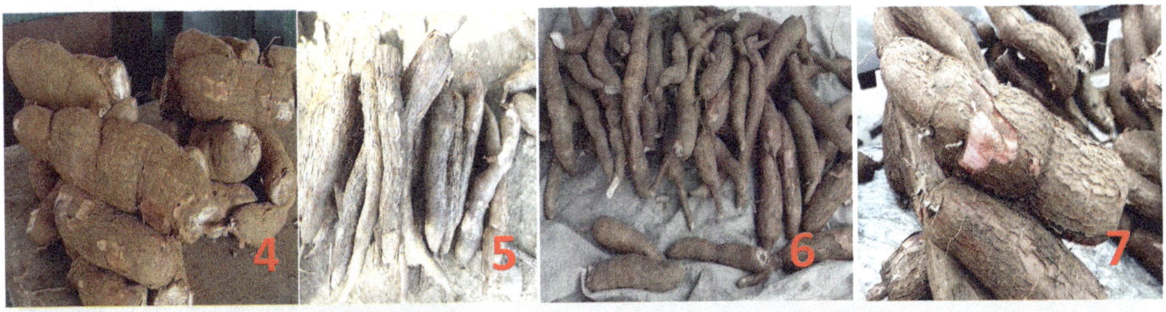

Physical differences of Tubers of Cassava varieties.

The photos of the Cassava roots/tubers above were taken in markets in Buchanan and Monrovia. According to the market women, these are four different varieties. 4: Elephant; 5. "Take the word to the town." 6. Soft Cassava; & 7: Bassa Girl. 4 & 5 were taken in Buchanan (Grand Bassa). Their (4 & 5) names are translated from the local language, Bassa. Photos #6 & #7 were taken in Paynesville (Liberia). The seller described it as "Soft Cassava", a variety she says is good for roasting. Photo #7 is the well known Bassa Girl, a table variety. It is also soft and sweet. The seller told me that this particular variety was the "Red Bassa Girl"; and that there is also a "White Bassa Girl" variety. I did not know that. From looking at the tubers, can one tell how much starch and the quality you will get from the different varieties? No! A closer look at 4 & 7, you will notice some similarities. Are they the same or could it be a result of "cross-pollination", or they really do not know?

plants, sticks and tubers in the photos without reading the associated texts.

These photos on pages 56 and 57 are only meant to illustrate the physical appearances and differences between cassava varieties. It would be difficult for the inexperienced to identify a particular cassava variety just by looking at the stem, bark, leaf or root. As was said earlier, it is even a challenge for the experts.

Take a careful look at the photo on the right. You will notice two things. First, the tubers (roots) have different colors. One is darker than the other. This suggests that these might be two different cassava varieties. Secondly, there is some discoloration with what that looks like greyish rings (see the arrows) on the insides (meat) of the tubers. This cassava might be several days old after harvesting. The rings suggest some deterioration. These are some of the signs buyers should be looking for when purchasing cassava.

With time and experience you might be able to identify some of the more popular varieties. In the meantime, it is best to leave it to the real, certified and experienced experts- the people at CARI and the experienced cassava farmers. In most cases you will just have to accept their word for it. Do not worry, the farmer, in most cases, will not deceive you, I am sure this will also apply in other cassava growing countries.

As for the particular substance a particular variety produces, unfortunately, one cannot tell this just by looking at the cassava variety. This will not provide any information. Actually, all cassava produces the same substance, starch. So, technically, what we really want to know is the quantity and quality of the starch and the amount of cyanide a particular variety produces. It is whole process that involves various steps. For this publication, we are not going into this because it is quite complicated. You will have to rely on information from research institutions like CATAS and IITA and your own national research institutions. There is no intention to make this difficult. This is just how it is.

Experience and experiment are going to be your best teachers. In the process of writing this guide, I have learnt a lot, and I am still learning. As I was in the process of my final editing exercises of the guide, I came across several varieties I have not seen before. Some I have listed, described and discussed in this section. But a few days ago, I came across a few new ones. The photo above is one of those varieties. See the colour of the stems and how tall it is.

Selecting the right Cassava variety to plant

In addition to the physical differences between cassava varieties, there are also differences in what each variety produces. What were illustrated in the last section are, basically, the physical appearances of the cassava plant, which are readily identifiable by sight, not the substance (starch) the cassava produces. Remember what we said in the beginning about growing the variety that will give you the substance you want? When you are selecting the variety you want to plant, the variety (planting material) you select should be based on what you would like to produce and the quantity you want to produce. In fact, the illustration provided by the photos on the previous pages, including the roots (tubers), which also have different physical appearance, characteristics and colour does not provide any information on substance.

If you want to produce Gari, you will have to select the variety that is best for Gari (Farina). If you want to produce starch, then you need to select the variety that will give you high quantity of starch. For industrial purposes, select the variety that is best for that purpose. I think you got the idea. There is not much that can be said here because for most of us who grow cassava, we will select what is available. And in most cases, it does work for our purposes. When you start to industrialize, well, that is a completely different story, and it is where the challenges begin.

Technically, the cassava variety we plant should be based on what we want to produce, especially if we are producing for a client who has specific needs. For someone, who needs and specifically requires the Yellow Root variety, this is what you should plant. Do not mix that variety with another variety and try to pass it on to the customer. It will destroy your business. If your client wants the Yellow Root, not only is it a must that you look for and acquire the *Yellow Root* variety, but you must also be aware of the production requirements of that variety, including, how to plant it and when to harvest it. In the case of the *Yellow Root*, it should be matured and harvested at nine months after planting.

Again, *Table 2* on Page 46 does provide some guidance. This table is from the *Liberia Cassava Feasibility Study*. An updated table listing 31 varieties has been provided by the *Roots and Tuber Division* of CARI. It is in Appendix 4 (pages 144 & 145). This list is quite detailed with a bit more information. Perhaps, in the future information on starch quantity will be available also.

In this publication there is much mentioned about the work of CARI, CATAS, IITA and other research institutions. Much of the work at these research institutions is dedicated to developing newer, disease-free and highly productive cassava and other crops varieties. We will discuss cassava diseases and the pests that are responsible for these diseases and viruses. I would like to stress here that not all of the work at these institutions are limited to creating disease-free (or desease-resistant) varieties. Some of the work is on focused creating varieties that can grow in other climatic zones other than the ones that plants normally grow in. While other activities are concentrated on creating more nutritious crop varieties. In fact, one could dedicate an entire chapter or book to the work scientists and cassava breeders do at these institutions, which, in most cases are very complex. For now, we would like to focus on the work they do to create more productive varieties,

In the beginning of this Guide, it was mentioned that one of my motivations for writing the Guide was my experience in China at the Chinese Academy of Tropical Agriculture Sciences (CATAS) in the *Cassava Production and Processing Training for African Countries*. The training received at CATAS was very special because, even though, it was mainly focused on cassava, we were exposed to other aspects of the work of CATAS, which not only complimented our training but also exposed us to some of the other important work of the academy. We had the opportunity to see the important works of the National Bamboo Institute, the National Coconut Institute; and we also were able to observe some of the efforts that were being undertaken in the development of the Chinese rubber industry, which at that time was in its infancy.

At the National Coconut Institute, we got to see the important work of biological control, which was being carried out to control the insects that affect the growth of coconuts; and many of the products that are being developed from coconuts, including, food, cosmetics and furniture. In fact, it would be good to note here that the Chinese told us that their work in biological control was influenced by similar work from Nigeria. At the Bamboo institute, we got to also see new innovations in creating value added bamboo products, including clothing, furniture and craft.

The works at institutions like CARI, CATAS and IITA are done for you, the farmer and would-be entrepreneur, because these are the places where you will eventually get the varieties that will allow you to produce what you want; and that will allow your business to be profitable. With the looming climatic and environmental crises, we cannot afford to cultivate large tracks of land anymore just to produce the quantities we want. We have to produce more on less land with less or no fertilizers, pesticides and harmful agrochemicals to control insects, pests and their associated diseases. The research work of the scientists and plant breeders at these research institutions are dedicated to achieving this.

The group of photos on the next page (61) are illustrations of some of the activities and technologies African participants at the CATAS training were introduced to; and the ones on page 62 illustrate some of the important work being carried out by cassava scientists and breeders of the Roots and Tubers Division of CARI at Suakoko (Bong County, Liberia). In the case of CARI, farmers and producers can purchase cassava cuttings directly from the institution.

Photos from CATAS Cassava Production and Processing Training Technology for African Countries
In photo 1, participants doing laboratory work. In Photo 2, Participants in field study with Prof. Dr. Huange of CATAS.; Photo 3: artificial pollination project of author at CATAS; Photo 4: author with other participants transplanting germplasms; Photo 5: Participants conducting laboratory work. Photo 6: Measuring Cassava starch content. (Photos taken by author's camera using timer.)

Photos from CARI's Roots and Tuber Division of Department of Crops

Photo 1: Butter Cassava variety. Photo 2. Mercy Lah, a Cassava scientist, showcasing a bumper harvest of one of the improved varieties. Photo 3: One of the improved varieties being developed. Photo 4: Harvested cassava of another improved variety (see the tag). Photo 5: CARI Cassava researchers with workers preparing Ridges in the field. Photo 6: the 0/357 improved variety. 31 varieties are listed in the Appendix (Appendix 4, page 139) with their various characteristics, including yield per hectare. (Photos courtesy of CARI)

Storing Planting Material

At this point, I am assuming that you have acquired your planting materials or are in the process of collecting them and will need to store them for use later. Now, I will assume that you are asking yourself, "How do I know how many cassava sticks I should buy?" This is a very good question, and you will get the answer shortly. Do not worry about this. I suggest that you read the entire guide before you actually start planning, or as you plan your project. However, for your information, the actual size of your plot and the spacing you use between each plant will determine the quantity of cassava cuttings or number of cassava sticks you will need.

This is not the way to store Cassava sticks.

This will be a good time to consider the differences between cassava cuttings and cassava sticks. Basically, the two terms are used interchangeably, however, it is important for you to know that, technically, there is a difference; and you the cassva farmer should know this.

Actually, the cassava stick is what you get the cuttings from. The cuttings or stems are what you actually plant. Sticks can be as long as 1.5 meters depending on the variety. And cuttings or stems are generally 25-30 cm (10"-12"). Based on this, one can calculate that you can get an average of 4 (four) cuttings from one cassava stick. This is the formula or yardstick that is used to calculate the number of cuttings one would get from a bunch or bundle of cassava sticks. Of course, this is dependent on the number of sticks in the bunch.

Storing cassava sticks under a tree is better.

Normally, in Liberia, there are 50 (fifty) sticks to a bunch. In the photo above, you can see that these cassava sticks are tied in a bunch. If you look carefully, you also see that the sticks are of different lengths. This is how cassava sticks look before they are cut into the shorter cuttings (or stems). The photo on the next page illustrates what cuttings (stems) look like after they have been cut and prepared for planting.

At this time, the information that you need to have, is that you must do everything possible to acquire your cassava cuttings or sticks well in advanced of the time you actually plant. Because, as was said earlier, you do not want to go through the trouble of land acquisition and preparation and do not have the sticks or cuttings available when you need them the most. The actual chore of preparing the cuttings can be done at planting or just before. Yes, the cuttings have to be prepared for planting.

Having dealt with this, it is also very important to note that when we talk about preparing cassava cuttings for planting, it is not limited to just cutting the stems to a certain length. Actually, it could be more than that. In some cases, to control the incidence of diseases, cuttings have to emerge in some solutions which can help to prevent the introduction of diseases in the field. In the case of using a mechanical planter, the cuttings have to be prepared according to the requirement of the particular planter you are using.

Having said this, let us deal with the issue of storing our cassava sticks for later use. The best and safest way to store your cassava sticks is to stand them up under a shade where the ground is damp. Storing them under a tree or against the wall under the eaves of a house in an area where there is not going to be any direct sun light on the sticks, is highly recommended. The idea is to keep the hot sun off the sticks- the planting materials. The heat from the sun will dry them up if you do not store them in the shade.

I do not care where you have seen it been done, do not lay them on the ground. Yes, I know, your people and mine have been laying them on the ground as far back as you can remember. But as I have said, our people do have very good knowledge on cassava; but there has been a lot of research done also, and the information provided here is based on both experience and research. Stand the sticks up. Standing them up allows them to draw moisture from the ground which keeps them moist and fresh.

We are not going to talk about preparing the sticks for planting just yet. I know what you are thinking, "What do you mean by, 'Cassava sticks have to be prepared?'" Yes! They must be prepared and prepared properly, but we will get to that later. In the main time let's discuss something very important. I know you are anxious to start planting, but this is an informative guide. So, let us have a little patience. If you do not want to lose your planting materials (Cassava sticks) and your valuable investments store the sticks as recommended in a cool shaded area, under the eaves of a house, or under a tree standing them up as illustrated in the photo at the bottom of page 63. Do not lay them down on the ground in the open as is illustrated in the photo at the top of page 63.

Cassava Planting methods

As you source your planting material and are preparing to plant, it is important for you to know that cassava can be planted in several different ways. Traditionally, our people plant cassava by digging a rectangular hole about 4" x 12" x 4" (four inches by twelve inches by four inches deep) as illustrated in the photo below. Three to four sticks (cuttings) are placed in the hole and covered with dirt. In Lofa County (Liberia), farmers use as many as six sticks. This is done randomly in the field without any order. However, with new information based on extensive research, this way of planting Cassava is being discouraged. In fact, it is not recommended planting cassava this way anymore.

Traditional way of planting.
*(Photo from **Liberia Cassava Feasibility Study**)*

Our people have been planting cassava this way for generations; and as with farmers everywhere in the world, trying to change their planting habits or way of farming can be very difficult, but we are getting there. Farmers have their reasons for planting the way they do, and it has worked for them over the years, but we are trying to increase their productivity and income, and also save them time and money. So, the old way of planting cassava is not recommended anymore. There are several reasons why the old method is not recommended and being discouraged, but two of the most important reasons are that it is not very productive, and it is very wasteful.

It is not necessary to use more than one cutting (cassava stick). In fact, in Grand Kru County (Liberia), farmers just lay the sticks on the ground. They do not even bother to cover them with dirt. Sounds crazy, but that is the way they have been planting cassava for generations. For them, it works. However, you (and they) can get better yields if cassava is planted using one of the newer modern planting methods.

Basically, there are three ways or methods of planting cassava. The three ways include the traditional method with a slight adjustment (only one cutting is used). This is referred to as the ***horizontal*** or ***flat*** *method*. The other two are the ***mound*** and the ***ridge*** methods. We will look at all three ways (methods) of planting cassava with their benefits and drawbacks in detail. The other thing that must be noted here, which is very important and must be employed with all three methods, is that the planting field must be properly prepared, measured and laid out properly. Things cannot be random anymore. There must be order with some degree of uniformity and accuracy (as much as possible).

After the three methods are explained in detail, you will understand and appreciate why the planting area must be well prepared, laid-out and de-stumped (if possible). For now let us just concentrate on some general information which you will need before actually planting the crop. The modern way of planting cassava is that the plants must be planted in line with 80-100 cm (0.08-1 meter) spacing between each plant, regardless which method you decide to use. We touched on this earlier.

Using the measurements given above for plant spacing gives uniformity, allows for better crop maintenance, increases production and a better quality produce. It also allows the producer to calculate exactly what the seed or planting requirements would be. This also allows better control and management of the field. The farmer can easily calculate average yield. For example, in a one-hectare plot planted with a spacing of 1m (one meter) a farmer would need 10,000 cassava cuttings (planting material).

*Please note that this is the general accepted standard– 10,000 cuttings per hectare. I also realize that you might be wondering why I am basing the calculation on the metric system's hectare in a country that uses the English system's acres. There are, basically, two reasons. One, all measurements in agriculture are shifting to the metric system; and two, the guide is meant for universal use. However, please do not be to concerned about this at this time. It will all become clear. Just read on.

That is if she is using one stem (cutting). If you plant the old way using three or more cuttings, the minimum amount of cuttings you will need for the same area would be 30,000. With that amount of cuttings you could plant three hectares. This is why we are stressing the use of one cutting. You can plainly see how much you will save. In the next section we will delve deeper into the three planting methods.

The Three Planting Methods in Detail

Finally! Now that we have acquired our cassava sticks and have stored them properly to be used when we are ready to plant, let us now take a closer look at the different planting methods. The actual cutting preparation could also take place as we plant. Honestly, we could have done this earlier, but I chose to do it this way because once we get the information and decide which method to use, the next stage would be is to actually start planting the crop.

Now, let us take a look at the planting methods in more detail with their benefits and drawbacks (constraints). As we said above, there are three planting methods that are used today, or to be honest, are being promoted. I am sure many of our farmers are still using the old traditional random way of planting cassava. The three methods are the ***Flat or Horizontal*** method, the ***Mound*** method and the ***Ridge*** method as we said above. So, let us now take a look at all three planting methods in detail.

1. The Flat/Horizontal or Traditional method:

This is just the same old traditional way of planting cassava but with a minor adjustment. Instead of using 3-4 cuttings in one hole, only 1 (one) is used as illustrated in the photo on the left. Few years ago farmers were being discouraged and advised not to use the old method of planting, and to adopt the newer ***mound*** or ***ridge*** method. Now, with some new information, which I am confident that the author of this guide had some influence in, farmers are now being advised and encouraged to use this ***one-stick flat or horizontal method.***[46] Of course, it must be done in line with proper spacing as indicated above. The eyes or growing points must all face one direction as indicated in the illustration at the bottom of the next page. Please note that it is also recommended to use one cutting in the other two methods.

The newer Flat/Horizontal Method

Advantages:

The major advantages of using the newer one-stick Horizontal method are: it reduces wastage, increases production, and is less labour-intensive. Cassava cuttings are seeds, and farmers believe that the more sticks they plant, the better the chance that some-

[46] *At the training at CATAS, China, this is where this method (one stick horizontal) was taught and recommended. Before CATAS only the Mound and Ridge methods were being encouraged.*

thing will grow. They are also concerned about pests, particularly termites, whatwe call bugabug. The rationale is, "If we plant two or more stems, the termites will eat (destroy) one or two, and the others will grow." The first thing for us to know here is that though cassava sticks are indeed seeds from which the cassava plant grows, the eyes or ribs on the stems, which I like to call *growing points*, are the real seeds or *points* from where the roots are established. So, actually a 12" (30-35 cm) cassava stem or cutting has several *growing points*. Having more than one cutting also increases competition for food and nutrients. The picture above is an illustration of a cassava cutting with several pits (see arrows pointing) or growing points. These pits are where the individual cassava plants will sprout from.

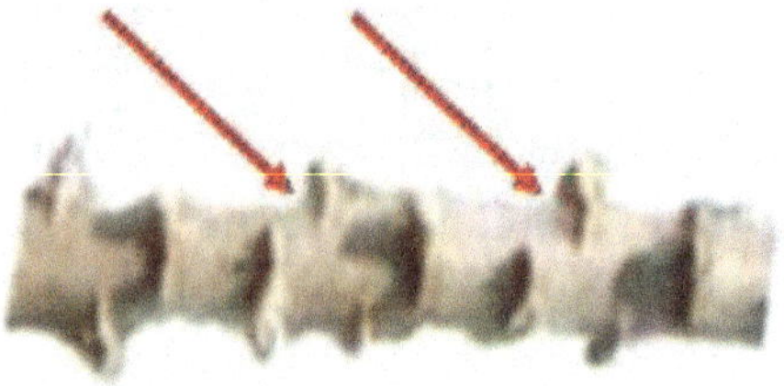

A Cassava cutting.

When I talk to farmers about using one cutting instead of the three or four they are used to planting, I always compare this to having several persons trying to eat one bowl of rice together. I always ask the farmers this question: "Don't you think one or two persons will always eat more than the others?" With this comparison, the farmers seem to understand and get the message. However, they are very right on the issue of pests, particularly, termites. The issue of termites should be addressed at the land acquisition and preparation stages. You, the farmer, must examine, very carefully, the land you want to plant cassava on to see whether there are termites on it. It is not that difficult to see signs of termites. All you have to do is look for the termites' hills.

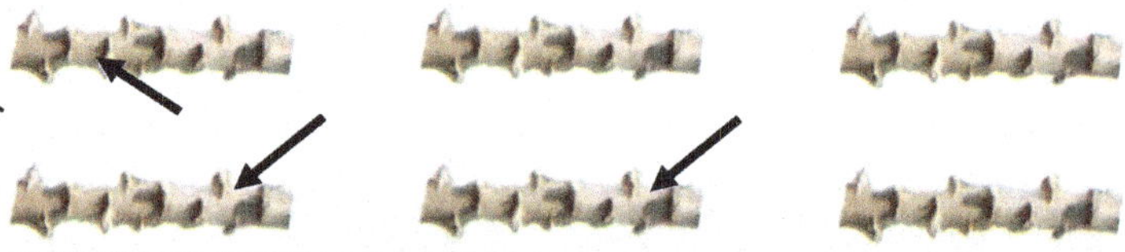

Flat/Horizontal Method

Take a care look at the illustration above. What do you see? All the ribs/pits (see arrows) are going in the same direction. This how the cuttings should be planted in Flat/Horizontal method.

Constraints:

The major constraints for the Flat/Horizontal method are the field must be laid out and measured properly which can be labor-intensive and expensive. Again, the land should be de-stumped.

2. The Mound method

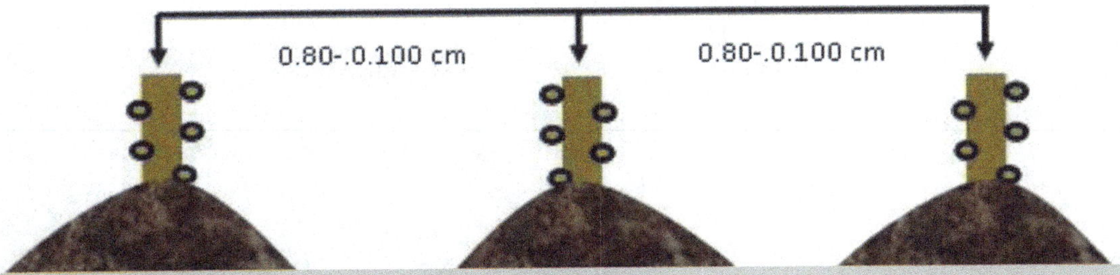

An illustration of the Mound Method. See how the mounds are built and the Cassava cuttings are placed in the mounds.

In the mound method, a hole is dug, and dirt is piled up as if you were planting yams, but the hole does not have to be as large or as deep as with yams. The main purpose for digging the hole is to loosen up the ground and soil. One single cutting is inserted at least six to eight inches into the mound with the eyes (ribs) of the cassava stick facing up. Some cassava experts recommend that cuttings be placed at a 45^0 (forty-five degree) angle; and some also use two cuttings. Even though, I do not recommend it, you can plant at 45^0, if you want to experiment, but I do not recommend using more than one cutting. It has the same result as the older traditional method, wastage.

Photo of an example of the one-stick Mound method.

Remember proper spacing (0.80-1.0 m) must be maintained also. These spacing specifications apply to all three method. Please note that 0.80 m is 80 cm (eighty centmeters). If you use 80 cm- spacing you will require more cuttings- 12,000 (twelve thousand).

Benefits:

Increased production and easier to manage.

This is what a well-planted Mound field should look like. The plants are uniformly planted and spaced. There is enough space to allow you to walk trough the plants. It provides enough space between the plants for intercropping.

Constraints:

The mound method is labour-intensive. This is a lot of work, period. It is a bit more Expensive to prepare; but it could be well worth it with the increased yields and ease of maintenance. If you decide to use the Mound meth od, remember that the field must be planted before the heavy rains or the soil will be washed away and the cuttings will also be exposed.

Take a careful look at the two photos at the bottom of the page. These are photos of two fields planted using the Mound method. In addition to what has been pointed out in the caption, the soil seems to have been washed way in the field in the photo on the left. This field must have been planted just before a heavy rainfall or not long before one. If you are going to use the mound method, you must plant before the heavy rains to a allow your plants roots to take hold of the soil. Remember to plant at least 2 to 3 weeks be fore the Rainy Season.

Caution when planting with the Mound Method

The photos above shows two separate fields. Both farmers used the Mound method, but what do you see? Look at the one on the left- the spaces between the plants are not uniformed compared to those in the photo on the right. In fact, the plants in the photo on the left are wide apart and lack order and uniformity. You can also see that some of the soil has been washed away, and there are puddles. This is what you must try your very best to avoid. The field on the right is clean, and you can see that the canopy is beginning to form. It could be better. The plants could have been a bit closer to each other, but it is not bad. Honestly, it looks like a combination of Mounds and Ridges.

3. The Ridge Method

An illustration of the Ridge method.

The ridge method is not very different from the mound method, but instead of mounds you build ridges. After building the ridges, you insert one cutting on each side of the ridge as is illustrated in figure above. I do not recommend that you use this method except you have a tractor or a Power Tiller equipped with ridging capability. However, if you have the money and manpower, you can go ahead and use it. It will also work well.

Benefits:

The benefits of the Ridge method are the same as with the other two methods, increased production and easier crop management and maintenance. However, the ridge method when done properly could provide better irrigation, and water management. In addition, it also might be the best method for intercropping.

Constraints:

Very labour-intensive, and in most cases will requires a tractor or power tiller with ridging capability, which could be costly.

All three of these methods when done properly will provide increased yields, better crop management, and weed control. They also provide something else: better intercropping. We will look at intercropping and its benefits later.

Fields of Ridges

These are examples of a mechanized-built ridges. The photo on the left was built by a tractor drawn ridger. The ridges are flatter and the trenches are shallow. The photo on the right is a field being prepared with a Power Tiller equipped with a ridger. (Photo on the right courtesy of CATAS.)

The Photos above are more examples of ridging.
Photo 1: Farmers planting cassava in a Ridged field. Please observed how they are planting the cassava stems.
Photo 2: Tractor-drawn cassava planter with ridging capabilities - see the attached ridgers (arrows).
(Photos, Courtesy of CATAS.)

Laying out the field for planting and the tools needed

Now that we have discussed the three new ways or methods of planting cassava in some detail, and understand how cassava is planted using them, it is time to get to work and start preparing to plant. That is assuming that we have made the decision on which method to use. Having made the decision, the next thing to do is start laying out our field or planting area. To do this we will need some tools.

Yes, indeed, we are going to need some tools for the job. I am sure, some of the same tools were listed earlier in other parts of the guide; and I am sure that you might even have some on hand. But now as you can tell, that as we layout the planting area, we have to have some degree of accuracy. Why? Because we are going to be planting the cassava field according the plant spacing we have decided to use. So, we need to do some measurements, and we need to be accurate in our measurement as much as possible.

Remember, we are not going to be planting cassava randomly anymore. We are going to be planting in an orderly and more technical and scientific manner. So, in addition to the regular tools (hoe, cutlass, shovel, digger, rake, etc.), you will need tools that will allow you to make the required measurements which will give you some degree of accuracy and uniformity based on your plant spacing. In order to achieve this, you will need the following:

- Tape rule/measuring tape (at least 100 meters long)
- Line/string
- Shovel
- Sticks/pegs
- Mallet or hammer
- Small hoe or digger
- Patience

Some of the tools needed for laying out the field.

It should be obvious why we need a tape rule; but a 100-meter length? Well, you could get something shorter in length and cheaper, but it would be time-consuming when measuring long distances, and we must also keep thinking in the future. What if we decide to expand our project to a hectare or above? Then the 100 m measurement tape is a must; but a 100 yard (30 m) tape will work just fine.

The *line* is used to maintain some degree of accuracy and uniformity. It is used with the pegs to layout the field. The field will not be 100% exact, but the line will give you and your workers a marker to follow.

The *sticks* or *pegs* are used with the line, and they serve as markers for the spacing between plants.

The *mallet or hammer* is used to punch the pegs into the ground; and finally, you will need *patience,* particularly with your workers, to complete the job.

If the field is laid out properly, it will make it easier to calculate the number of cuttings you would need and prevent wastage.

The illustration below is of a field being laid out. Do you see the sticks (Black Arrows) and the twine (White Arrows)? See how the distance between the twine (rope) is even. This is a very good example of how one should lay out the field.

A cassava field being laid out. See the twine and pegs. (Courtesy, NCSCC)
The black arrows point to the peg/sticks and illustrate the width (0.80 m—1 m). The white arrow point to the twine, which also identify the length of the field. There should be pegs/sticks or some markers also along the line to demarcate plant insertion points (0.80-1 m) spacing..

Calculating Planting Material Needed

Now it is time to calculate the amount of seeds, or in the case of cassava, cuttings/ stems, you would need for your project - actually, for this particular field. I am sure you are asking yourself, "How did you arrive at the figure (10,000) in the "Planting Method" section on page 66?" It is very simple, and I will try our best to explain it in detail in this section. The calculations that was made in that section, and the ones that will be made in this section are based on the Metric System's hectare, and the plant-spacing we decide to use. Once you understand how to calculate for a hectare, you will be able to calculate seed requirements for smaller plots, including, for the English system of lots and acres.

In our system of measure, we normally use the English system of measurement- ***inches***, ***feet***, ***yards*** and ***mile*** for length; and ***lots*** and ***acres*** for land area measurements; ***pound*** and **tons** for weights; and ***quart*** and ***gallon*** for liquid measurements. But things have changed, and almost all measurements in agriculture are done using the metric system.

The metric system uses ***centimeter*** (cm), ***meter*** (m), ***kilometer*** (km) for length; ***hectare*** (ha) for land area measurements; ***gram, kilogram*** (kg), and metric tonne (MT) for weights; and the ***liter*** for liquid measurements. It is not that simple. The units of measurements can be further broken down into smaller units in both the English and metric systems. But for now let us just focus on the units we will generally use in most of our daily agricultural activities. We are not trying to and neither do we want to be very technical here. We just want to provide information that will make life simple.

As was said earlier, in agriculture, the metric system of measurement has basically replaced the English system, even here in Liberia. Why? Because it is lot easier to use, it is universal, and it is widely used across Africa. Cocoa farmers and exporters, in Liberia, measure their cocoa in kilograms (kg) and rice farmers measure their plots by meters (m). Our farmers who live near the borders with Guinea, the Ivory Coast and Sierra Leone are very familiar with the metric system and so too are our cross-border traders. Even some vegetable sellers in Monrovia use the metric system, especially, kilos (kilograms) to measure their produce. The vegetable sellers on Benson Street, one of the major vegetable markets in Monrovia (Liberia) measure their goods primarily in kilos.

The metric system is quite simple to use once you understand it. For example, 1 (one) hectare is 10,000 m^2 (square meters), as was said previously. As was explained in the earlier section, if you decide to use a spacing of 1.0 m (100 cm) between plants you would need 10,000 cuttings. How do we know this? Because we already know that our one hectare plot is 10,000 m^2 (ten thousand square meters). To find out how many cuttings would be needed for this one hectare-plot, we simply divide ten thousand square meters by one square meter ($10000^2/1^2$). Our answer will be 10,000. Therefore, the one -hectare plot would need 10,000 cuttings. This is the beauty of working with the metric system. It is simple.

Now, let us go a bit deeper into this because things could be a bit complicated. Supposed you decide to use a different plant spacing than the standard one meter-spacing, how would calculate for the number of cuttings you would need? The first thing that you need to know or remember, is that 1 ha (hectare) is one hectare. And that one hectare is 10,000 square meters (10000 m^2). So, now that we understand this, we can now do the necessary calculations for any plant-spacing.

So, let us calculate for a 80 cm (0.80 m) plant spacing. Since we have 10,000 square meters, we will be using 0.80 m plant spacing, we will square the 0.80 m. That is, we will multiply 0,80 by .080 (0.80 x 0.80). This will give us 0.64 m^2 (0.64 square meters). Next, we divide 10000 $m^2 \div 0.64$ m^2 ($10000 \div 0.64$). The answer will be 15,625. This is the number of cuttings you will need for this plant spacing. If you want to know the number of cuttings (stems) you will need for any plant spacing, you will do the same calculations.

So, what if we decided to use the IITA recommended spacing (100 m x 0.80 m)? Let us do it step by step:

Step 1: Multiply: $0.80 \times 1.0 = 0.80$ m^2
Step 2: Divide: 10000 $m^2 \div 0.80$ m^2 (The m^2 will cancel out and we go to Step 3.)
Step 3: Simply and divide: $10000 \div 0.80 = 12{,}250$
Therefore for this plant spacing, you will need 12,250 cuttings.

With this knowledge and an understanding of the basic principles in these calculations, a farmer can calculate for many things in her various farming activities. She can not only calculate her seed needs, but she can also estimate what the plot or farm will produce. That is in yield.

To estimate the quantity her farm will produce, all the farmer has to do is harvest a portion of the farm, and she would be able to calculate potential yield.

As an example, let us take a look at the illustration on the left at the top of the next page which represents one hectare of planted cassava. Notice that the plot is clearly measured 100 m x 100 m, representing 10000 square meters, 1 ha (one hectare), as illustrated by the figure. Suppose we cut out a 10 m by 10 m (100 m^2) portion (represented by the shaded area in the illustration) of the farm and harvest it. This 100 m^2 (one hundred square meters) portion would represent 1% (one per cent) of the total farm or plot. How did we arrive at this? Simple! We divided 100 m^2 (the harvested portion) by 10,000 m^2 (the entire farm). *That is [$100^2 \div 10000^2$ ($100 \div 10{,}000$) = 0.01].* This gives us 0.01 (1%). I know all of us are not math students, but just follow. You will get it.

Next, we would weigh the entire harvest from the portion of the plot we cut out (harvested). Supposed the cassava harvested from this portion is weighed at 25 kg? That means that 1% (one percent) of the farm produced 25 kg of cassava. In order to estimate what the total production of the farm would be, we multiply 100 (which represents the entire farm (100%) by 25 kg (100 x 25) which would give us 2,500 kg or 2.5 MT. Our one-hectare plot is supposed to produce 2.5 metric tons according to our calculations.

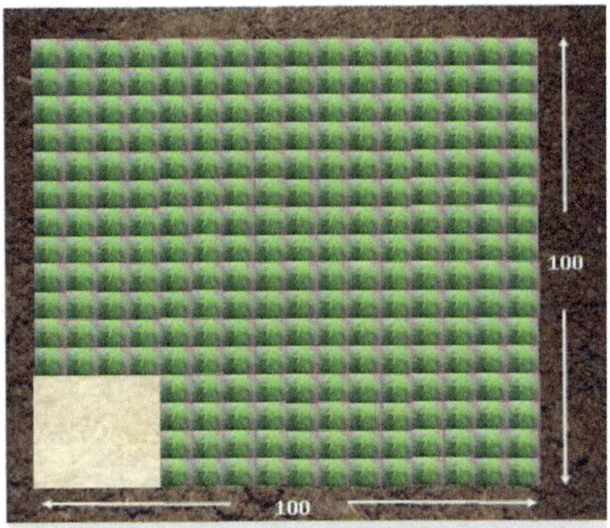

A 100 m x 100 m (one hectare) cassava plot with an area cut out.

On the first look, I know this might look a bit difficult, but once you get a good understanding of the metric system and learn how to do these calculations, you will appreciate it. You will also be able to calculate your seed requirements and potential yield for any crop, not just for cassava. Please note that these are just estimates. Yields could be lower or much higher. Remember we have pests, unforeseen weather conditions and of course, theft. All of these things can adversely affect yield. Theft is a major problem and something that you should not only be aware of, but you should do all you can to try to control and prevent.

With this knowledge, it is easy to see that we can calculate seed cost and a whole lot of other costs, including labour cost. And most importantly, we could very well estimate the value of our project as was demonstrated above.

For example, supposed cassava is selling at $25 (twenty-five US dollars) per ton. In our first scenario, at 10% of our farm, the estimated value of the farm would be at about $62.50 per hectare. Now I know what's going on in your mind, "All that work?" Please do not panic. The figures used in this illustration are just to make the process easier to understand. Your yields and the price you receive for your cassava could be higher. It all depends on the size of your project and the price of cassava at the time of harvest. It is hoped that your project would be much larger than one hectare, and that you will have greater yields. Just remember yields are not only determined by land size alone. Proper land preparation, plant variety, plant management and maintenance, and fertilizer-use can contribute to higher yields and hopefully, higher incomes. I met a farmer is Tanzania who told me that he was getting as high as 80 tons per hectare. And in Nigeria, there are farmers who are getting up to 40 tons per hectare also. You too can get these same results or even higher if you put the time and effort into your project and follow the recommendations that are being provided in this Guide.

Calculating Planting Material Cost

Regardless which planting method you use, the cost of planting material will basically be the same. Why? Because the planting method you use, does not affect the cost of planting material. The people who sell planting material do not sell them based on planting method. The total cost of the planting material for your field is determined by the plant spacing you decide to use between the plants and the size of your plot. Remember, we said that the spacing between plants should be between 0.80 - 100 cm (0.80 -1 meter). This is uniform and applies to the three planting methods. So, what you finally pay for planting material for your entire field will depend on the plant spacing you decide to use. If you use 80 cm plant-spacing you will need more cuttings compared to a 100 cm (one meter) plant-spacing. This will become clearer later.

Actually, the only cost that could be different would be the cost of laying out the field, which includes labour and equipment, especially if you employ mechanization. And this will depend on the method you decide to use. All three planting methods require labour. However, labour cost will vary depending on the method you use and the associated labour requirement; and the labour cost in the part of the country where your land is located.

As was discussed earlier, it is very important that you start sourcing planting materials before you get into the details of land preparation and laying out your field. There is no use of going through all of the trouble, and when it comes time to plant, you do not have the planting material you will need for your project. The worst that could happen is that you may have more cuttings than what you would need. It is like building a processing plant without first identifying where you will get your raw materials from. You might end up with a beautiful and well-equipped factory without anything to process.

Normally, Cassava sticks are sold by the bunch,[47] except you purchase them from an institution like CARI or a producer who sells pre-cut 35 cm (12 in) cuttings in smaller bunches of fifty cuttings. These pre-cut cuttings normally cost at about $5 (five US dollars) per bunch of 50 (fifty) cuttings. Majority of our farmers buy planting materials by the larger bunch and cut them to the required size themselves. I will assume that, in most cases, this is how you are going to get your cassava cuttings yourself. The inset on the bottom of the next page provides estimates of the quantity of cuttings you will need per hectare based on the three spacing specifications: 0.80 cm; 0.90 cm and 100 cm (1.0 m). These are just the basic rules you can follow. However, regardless of which specification you decide to use, you can always make adjustments.

The other information the inset provides is an estimate of what it might cost you to purchase pre-cut cuttings. The cost could be higher or lower. It depends on where and who you buy the cassava sticks or cuttings from.

---

[47] *In Liberia Cassava sticks are sold by the "Bunch'. In Nigeria and some other African countries, the standard is "Bundle".*

The inset also provides information on what planting material might cost for one hectare planted using one the three recommended plant-spacing. However, please note these estimates are based on a set standard (US$5 per bunch of cuttings) to make your calculations easy and simple. However, based on where you purchase your cuttings from, your cost could be a lot lower. I think with this information we can now move to the next topic: Cutting Preparation.

Cutting needs per hectare:

The current trend for planting cassava whether one uses the Flat, Mound or Ridge method is to plant one cutting at a space of 0.80-1.00 meter. Based on this, the required cuttings required for each plant spacing are listed below:

- *At 0.80 meter the cuttings required for one (1) hectare is 15,625.*
- *At 0.90 meter the cuttings required for one (1) hectare is 12.345.*
- *At 1.0 meter the cuttings required for one (1) hectare is 10,000 .*

Determining the number of bunches needed to plant one hectare.

- *Normally there are 50 sticks to 1 bunch of cassava sticks.*
- *One stick is approximately one (1) meter long (not uniformed, could be longer or shorter).*
- *Each cutting is between 25-30 cm (about 12"). Therefore each cassava stick will provide 3-4 cuttings. Based on these calculations:*
    - ⇒ *one bunch of cassava stick will give between 150 to 200 cuttings. However, because of the irregular length of cassava sticks, one should calculate no more than 150 cuttings per bunch to be on the safe side.*
    - ⇒*for one hectare of cassava planted at 0.80 meter apart, one would need about 104 (one hundred and four) uncut bunches of cassava sticks.*
    - ⇒*for one hectare of cassava planted at 0.90 meter apart, one would need about 82 (eighty-two) uncut bunches of cassava sticks.*
    - ⇒*For one (1) hectare of cassava planted at 1.0 meter apart, one would need 67 (sixty-seven) uncut bunches of cassava sticks.*

Cost of cuttings:

- *The cost of a bunch of uncut cassava sticks varies across the county but generally ranges at LD$150-$300 (one hundred and fifty to three hundred Liberian dollars) per bunch, depending on location in the country.*
- *With the consideration of transportation cost, the general rule is one should calculate at US$5.00 (Five US dollars) per bunch.*
- *Therefore, based on the information above, the cost of cuttings for one (1) hectare of cassava will be as follows:*
    - ⇒*for 0.80m spacing: US$415 (four hundred and fifteen US dollars at US$5 per bunch of fifty cuttings*
    - ⇒*for 0.90m spacing: US$410 (four hundred and ten US dollars at US$5 per bunch of fifty cuttings)*
    - ⇒ *1 m spacing: US$335 (three hundred and thirty-five US dollars at US$5 per bunch of fifty cuttings)*

Cuttings preparation

I will assume that you have purchased your cassava sticks, by the bunch, of course. So, now we need to prepare them for onward planting. Except, you have purchased pre -cut cuttings. This would be good because you will not have the extra chore of preparing them. In this publication, I will assume that you have purchased the cassava sticks by the bunch, and they now have to be prepared for planting.

Notice the cutting's roundness and thickness.

Cuttings preparation is quite simple, and there is not any real need for a very long discussion. The only requirements are the proper tool and a relatively clean environment. The most important tool you need for this exercise is a very sharp cutlass or machete. I will also recommend that whether you use a cutlass or a machete, that it be sanitized.

You can use industrial alcohol or simply heat the cutlass or cutting tool to sanitize the cutlass. Sanitizing the cutlass will prevent diseases and viruses from being transferred to the cassava cuttings from other diseased varieties or from other sources and plants. Yes, cassava, like every other plant, does have diseases and viruses that affect it; and the truth is that most of our local varieties are diseased. I strongly recommend this (sanitizing) even though, it is not widely practiced by cassava farmers. I learned this from the Cocoa industry, and I think it can and should also be applied to cassava. Co-

This is a photo taken by the author while training farmers on how to prepare cuttings. Notice how the farmer places the stickon the ground gently. See the arrow pointing to the results of their work.

coa, like cassava, is also affected by various diseases that can adversely affect its production, both the quantity and quality.

The next thing to do is to select a soft spot on the ground where you can cut the cassava sticks without damaging them. You can also use some material, like grass or straw, to place the sticks on. This is very important because we do not want to bruise the cuttings, and we want a clean cut. Yeah! We must treat them delicately.

The cuttings must be cut at about 12 inches (about 30-35 centimetres) in length. The cassava sticks should be laid on the soft spot (or material) on the ground and a quick sharp blow be applied with the cutlass to the stick to give a rounded clean cut. Do not cut the sticks at an angle. Most cassava sticks are cut at one end at a 45° (forty-five degree) angle. Even though this is how most cassava sticks are cut, cutting cassava sticks this way is not recommended anymore.

Cassava stems/cuttings readied for planting

The cut should be rounded and smooth. This will give you good results. Take a look at the two photos on the previous page. The one at the top is an illustration of what the cutting should look like. The one at the bottom is of some farmers learning how to cut cassava sticks. Notice how the sticks are gently placed on the ground.

The group of photos below illustrate the three stages of cuttings/stems preparation. In stage one, the stems are cut to the appropriate length. In stage two, we compare cuttings in size and thickness; and finally, in stage three, we select the most appropriate cutting for planting. Look at the two cuttings in the photo in the middle. The one on the left is not only shorter, but it is thin. You could plant it, but the one on the right will give you better results.

3-stage cuttings/stems preparation.

Stage 1. Cut stems to the appropriate length. Stage 2. Compare stems. Stage 3. Select appropriate stem.

Selecting which Planting Method to Use

Now, that we have a pretty good understanding of the various planting methods, their benefits and challenges, and have learned how to prepare the planting material (cuttings), it is time to plant. Your next question might be, "Which method should I use?" This is a very good question, but it is not very easy for me to give you an answer. Why? Because I cannot make the decision for you. The decision must be yours and be based on your particular situation and your understanding of the various planting methods, their benefits and challenges. What might work for me might not work for you. I guess this is where we have to do a *cost benefit analysis*.

What I would say is, that in most cases, I would recommend the Flat/Horizontal method. Why? This is the traditional method our farmers have been using over the years, and even with the new ways of planting, it is easier and less labour-intensive than the other two methods, and it works very well if you use one cutting per hole. It should also be less expensive in terms of labour cost, and what you pay for planting material. But please remember, the cost of planting material (cuttings) will be determined by the plant spacing you decide to use between plants and the size of your plot.

What I would also recommend here, is that you look at your land and see what you think is best for you. There are many farmers who are using the both the Mound and Ridge methods, and they work for them, even though, they are labour-intensive. If you decide to use the Mound method, please remember to plant before the onslaught of the heavy rains because the soil might be washed away as the rainfall intensifies. As for the Ridge method, I would not recommend it except you have the proper equipment to build the ridges. However, if you have the money and the manpower to build the ridges, go ahead and give it a try. It would be money well-invested, and it is better for intercropping.

Time to plant

So, now that you have decided on which method to use, it is time to plant. Of course, by now you should have done your land preparation and hopefully, you have done the de-stumping as recommended. Yes, de-stumping is expensive and not absolutely necessary. However, in my opinion, there is no other way if you really want a real productive field that can be used year-to-year. It must also be noted that there are some experts who believe that leaving the roots and stumps in the field can be good for the plants. The rationale is that as the roots and stumps rot, they will provide needed nutrients.

This is true, but again, not to "Beat a dead horse!", if you can afford to de-stump, please do. Plants do regenerate. I have seen cassava fields with unnecessary plant growth everywhere; and remember what was said earlier, "Cassava does not compete well with other crops." And please do not forget, termites. They feed on dead and decayed wood and some live ones too. If you leave the dead roots in the field, you could well be providing food for the termites, and when that runs out, your cassava plants could be next.

In addition to this, another benefit of a well de-stumped field is that it would be lot easier and more effective to use a tractor or other mechanized equipment in the field in the future. Since we are at the planting stage, it is worth mentioning that there are tractor-driven cassava planters. They are not popular here, in Liberia and other parts of Africa, but they are available, and they can make life a lot easier. If we are going to industrialize the cassava industry, we need to plant larger fields; and we need to plant in the shortest of time. In order to do this, we will have no other choice than to employ mechanization in all aspect of cassava production, including planting. And therefore, mechanized cassava planters must be seriously considered. However, in order for them to be effective, your field must be de-stumped and free of unnecessary plant growth, above and below the grown. And you must have the right equipment. Just any size tractor will not work. You must have the right size to do the work. As was mentioned earlier, a 75 HP 4WD or above must be the standard.

In fact, this is not just an issue for cassava. This applies to other crops, especially rice and corn. The way we plant our crops, especially, cassava, corn (maize) and rice needs to be completely revisited. I am sure, you are asking, "I understand and know about rice and cassava, but why corn?" Corn is very important crop if we are going to develop our livestock and poultry industries. Corn is one the main ingredients for animal feed. Even though, this is a discussion for another time, but it is very important that it is mentioned here because once your cassava field is properly developed, who says that you cannot use it for another crop after harvest? As was suggested earlier, after you harvest your cassava field, you could plant something else in the field– perhaps groundnuts, corn or soy beans.

ESTABLISHING PLANTING AREA SIZE AND SEED NEEDS

At this junction, this is another time when we also need the tools (measuring tape, twine and pegs) mentioned and used in the section "Laying out the field for planting and the tools needed." Why? Because, the first thing that needs to be done at this time, is to establish the size of the plot. Actually, this exercise is not very different from what was done in that section, except that now we have to be a bit more detailed because this will determine how many cuttings we actually need. In that section and related exercise, we were, basically, just trying to layout the field to see what we actually had in space. Sounds confusing? I agree. But at that stage, we were just setting the groundwork for these activities - *establishing planting area size and seed needs.*

Now the issue or question is: "Is it an acre or a hectare or part there of?" I would suggest that we consider using the hectare as a benchmark or yardstick for measurement purposes, as was recommended earlier, even if we are just planting an acre or a smaller plot. Yes, I know, it is based on the metric system, and we are used to the English system's acres and lots, but believe me, the metric system is easier to work with, and it will make your job less complicated, and perhaps, your farming life a lot less hectic and easier.

Let us take another look at the metric system. We had discussed this earlier, but it is not a bad idea to revisit it and refresh our memory. The first thing you need to be reminded of, is that one hectare is equal to 2.5 (two and a half) acres or 10 lots; and one hectare is 10,000 m^2 (10,000 square meters). Remember? Again, it might sound like a lot but working in meters makes it easier to subdivide plots and calculate things like seed needs and yields once you have decided on the length of the spacing between plants that you would like to use. In some cases you might have to decide on both length and breadth. "Length and breadth?" You might ask. Yes, both length and breadth might have to be considered in your plant-spacing calculation. But do not panic. We will make this clear later.

No, I am not trying to make it more complicated. Cassava can also be planted in a not so uniformed pattern, like 100 cm x 100 cm or 90 cm by 90 cm. You can plant using two different plant-spacing. For example you can use 100 cm (length) one direction and 80 cm (breadth) in the other direction. Of course, you will need more cuttings. In fact, this plant spacing (100 cm x 80 cm) is also being recommended by IITA. Actually, it is not a bad idea. They are just trying to maximize the use of available land space. But for now, let us stick with the protocol (1 m x 1 m).

As was established earlier, in a one hectare plot you need 10,000 cuttings if you are using a planting space of 1m (100 cm)- that is 1 m between each plant or seedling. With this information you should be able to calculate your seed needs regardless of the size of your plot. Remember also, that if you use 80 cm between the plants you will need more than 10,000 cuttings.

So, supposed you only had one acre to work with, how do you establish how many cassava cuttings you are going to need? It is very simple. Since we already know that one hectare is equal to 2.5 (two and a half) acres, all you need to do, is to divide 10,000 by 2.5 (10,000÷2.5), and you will know that you will need 4,000 cuttings per acre (1,000 cuttings per lot). Remember that one acre has four lots in most cases.

I said *"in most cases"* because in Buchanan (Grand Bassa County, Liberia), where I am from, things are a bit different. In Buchanan there are five lots to one acre. Please do not ask me, "Why?" That is just how it is. So, if you are in Buchanan instead of 1,000 cuttings to a lot, it will be 800. Notice that the number of cutting per acre does not change. Why? Because an acre is an acre whether it is divided by four, five, or six lots.

Technically, if you were planting corn or pepper using the same spacing, you would also be able to calculate your seed requirements very easily. As was said earlier, once you know how to do this, you can calculate for any spacing you decide to use for any crop. Remember, that for cassava, your spacing can be 80 cm, 90 cm or 100 cm (1m), even though, the general standard is 100 cm (1 m).

Now, let's say you've decided to use 90 cm (0.90 m), what would be your cuttings requirements? One hectare is 10,000 square meters, right? So, first, we will multiply 0.90 by 0.90 (0.90 x 0.90). We will get 0.81. Then, we will divide 10,000 by 0.81 (10,000÷0.81) which will be 12,345.6. Therefore, we will need approximately 12,346 cuttings for one hectare. Again, if we want to know the quantity of seeds (cuttings), we need for the one acre, we simply divide 12,346 by 2.5 which will be about 4,938 cuttings per acre. From the calculation, it is obvious that you will need 2,346 (two thousand three hundred and forty-six) more cuttings than you would need if you were using the 100 cm (1 m) spacing.

The calculations above are straight forward and based on the plant-spacing specifications that have been universally recommended. However, you do not have to follow that to the letter. You can also adjust your plant spacing to 100 cm x 80 cm (1 meter by 0.80 m). This is the spacing used by IITA on its website.

Please remember that these spacing specifications are for cassava. The spacing for another crop could be more or less, but you can use the same principle.

For the fun of it, let us say that you were going to plant peppers on one acre of land next to your cassava, and you needed to purchase seedlings. How many seedlings would you need? We use seedlings here, instead of seeds, because of the nature of how peppers are grown.

Unlike cassava, corn and okra that are planted directly into the soil, with peppers, you have to set up a nursery. So, we expect that you will be purchasing your seedlings from a farmer who produces seedlings, except you want to go through the process and trouble of setting up a pepper nursery. That will be a completely different scenario which we are not going into. So, the assumption here is that you will be purchasing pepper seedlings from a farmer who develops nurseries and sells seedlings. And we hope so, because this is the value chain approach.

So, in ths case, the first thing you need to know is that the quantity of seedlings you would need will be determined by the plant-spacing between each pepper plant.[46] Right? Let us say that you decided on 40 cm (about 16 inches) spacing between the pepper plants. Now, based on what we have just learned, what would you do? You would first multiply 0.40 m by 0.40 m (0.40 x 0.40)which will give you 0.16 m^2. Then you divide 10,000 m^2 by 0.16 m^2. Why? Because we would first need to establish how many seedlings we need for one hectare. Once we find out what we need for a hectare, then we can calculate the seeds needed for both acres and lots. Please do not ask how we got 10,000?

Based on the information, let us see how many seedlings you will need for your one acre of peppers. First, we divide 10,000 square meters by 0.16 square meters (10000 ÷ 0.16). This gives us 62,500 (the amount of pepper seedlings needed for one hectare). Second, we divide 62,500 by 2.5. *(Remember, one hectare has two-and-a-half acres?)* This will give us 25,000. So, you will need 25,000 seedlings for the one acre. That was very easy. Was it not?

Suppose you decide that this amount of seedlings is too much and outside of your project's budget. So, you decide that instead of doing one acre, you decide to start with just one lot. Then to find out how many seedlings needed for the one lot, you divide the 25,000 by the number of lots that are in an acre in the area where you are located. So, if you are located somewhere in Montserrado County (Liberia) or elsewhere in Liberia other than Buchanan, Grand Bassa County, you should be dividing 25,000 by 4, right; and by 5, if you are in Buchanan, right? We will leave the rest of this calculation to you, because I think you have gotten the idea.

In the inset below, there is a brief note on the value chain approach.

In the value chain approach, or I may stress, that in an integrated value chain, we are supposed to buy and sell goods and services with and between each other (producers, manufacturers, farmers, sellers, etc.) within the particular sector's value chain. In this way everybody benefits, and the economy develops. While it is good to develop your own nursery or purchase your own equipment, however, if we want to develop the sector, then we, the actors within the chain need to share whatever resources we may have with others in the chain, giving them opportunities to sell to us what they produce, manufacture or markets; and they in turn, do likewise– buy from and sell to us. This is what is referred to as an Integrated Value Chain. Of course, in a fragmented value chain it is the other way around. Everybody does their own thing, and selfishness and greed prevails, and in the economy suffers and the value chain/sector does not grow.

Planting the crop

Now that you have made your decision on plant-spacing, selected the planting method you will use; and you have also selected the variety of cassava to plant, let us get busy and start planting. For this publication, we will use the newer **Flat/Horizontal** method, which, as was said earlier, is the traditional flat method with an adjustment. That one cutting is used, instead of the traditional three to four cuttings and plant our cassava in an orderly manner rather than randomly.

Yields of either of these new planting methods should be better than the old randomly -planted traditional method. However, if you are one of those farmers who have difficulties changing planting habits and want to be certain of the results you will get, you can plant the way you are used to. However, I will suggest that you plant smaller plots using the newer methods and compare yields. Just remember that, normally, most cassava varieties take up to nine and twelve months to fully mature. So, I suggest you experiment with one of the 3-6 month varieties, if they are available.

Another benefit of using one of the newer planting methods is that you will have a very nice, laid-out farm or field, in which you can easily walk through. There are other benefits also: intercropping and the ease of crop maintenance as was mentioned earlier.

So, we have followed all of the instructions, and now we are about to plant our field; but before we proceed, this will be good time and place to give some additional and perhaps, detailed information about planting cassava. The intention of this guide is to provide the reader with enough information that will allow him or her to be successful in their project. Some of the information that will be provided here and throughout the guide might have been mentioned earlier; and it might seem repetitive, but these things must be stressed to ensure success. I want you to succeed.

At this time you will need the measuring tape, pegs, twine and mallet. For the measuring tape and mallet it is not a big deal You already know what they are, and they should be very easy to get. In fact you can use a small hammer if you cannot find a mallet. However, I suggest that you do all you can to get the rubber mallet as is illustrated in the photo on the left. For the pegs and twine, it is another story, because what you would need will depend on the size of the plot you are planting. In this case, you will have to be quite creative and plan well. If you do not plan very well, you could end up spending a lot of money, and this is not what we want.

Remember, we are going be planting our field according to our planting measurements. If we go by the convention and try to lay out the entire field, we will need about the same amount of pegs (sticks) as cassava cuttings. Therefore, we need to lay the field out in stages, with smaller plots and use the pegs and twine as guides for the rest of the field. For example we could lay the field out in 20 m x 20 m plots. In this case we would need 400 pegs and 100 meters (30 yards) of twine. Better yet, we could subdivide the filed in half (100 m x 50 m) and just use the twine and pegs to set markers for the workers to follow. The main idea here is to plant the cuttings in line as straight and uniformed as possible. As was said above, this is the time for creativity and innovation, not shortcuts. At this critical junction, either you will have to supervise the process yourself or get someone you trust, and who knows what they are doing to manage the process. That is if you want a well-laid out planted field.

I am sure that, in most cases, pre-cut pegs might not be available, even though, they are manufactured in some countries. For us in Africa, especially in rural communities, we have to make the pegs ourselves from available materials, which I am sure would be plentiful in the area around the land you are planting in. The pegs could be made from either bamboo or sticks cut from trees in the area you are located. These are readily available and should not be expensive. The pegs should not be more than a foot-and-a-half in length with both flat and pointed ends. The pointed end can be cut at sharp 45^0 (forty-five degree) angle. This will allow it go into the ground smoothly.

At the bottom of Page 74 in the section, *"Laying out the field for planting and the tools needed"* there is a photo illustrating a field being laid out. This section also has a list of the tools need for laying out the field. They are the same tools you will be using at this junction. The only thing different that I would like to mention and remind you of in this section, is that do not plant different varieties of cassava within the same field in close proximity to each other.

Cassava Planting technology

The adage in agriculture is, *"What you put in is what you will get out."* In computer lingo, we say; *"Garbage in, Garbage out."* The same thing applies to agriculture, but this is not limited to the quality and amount of seeds. It depends on how well you prepare your field, and how well you plant the field. So, at this stage of the game, one should be very careful of not only what is put in the ground, but also, how it is put in the ground. Because at the end of the day you want to get (harvest) the most out of the hard work and money you invest in the project, even if it is just a backyard garden.

So, in this section, we will look at a couple of things: *planting specifications* (including cuttings size), and *when to plant.* At this time, if you have not prepared your cuttings, this will be the time to do so. Please refer to the section on *Cutting Preparation* and follow the instructions.

I. Planting specifications:[48]

- Stem must be sufficiently mature, woody and thick with short internodes (growing points), no empty pith, whole buds without injury, without pest and disease[49] and fresh (stem must have latex, or rich in water content).
- Cuttings should be between 15-20 cm (with 7-10 nodes), do not break or injure buds.
- Stems/cuttings should be from 8-12-month-old plants (will be difficult to know if not planted by you or purchased from a trusted source .)
- Stem size should be 1.5-2.5 cm (1/2"-3/4") diameter *oversize or thin sticks, and forked sticks are not good*
- Only one stick is used in the horizontal/flat method with eyes in the same direction.

Take a look at the photo above. See how thick the stem is, and the number of nodes (growing points) it has. This is what we want as per the specifications listed above.

When do we plant?

The time when cassava is planted is extremely important; and we must be very aware of this because it can really affect the results (yields) we get in the field. The recommendations here are based on:

- Training received at the Chinese Academy of Tropical Sciences (CATAS),
- Experiences here in our West African climatic conditions, and
- An ever-changing global climate.

---

48 *Based on CATAS training and recommendations*

49 *Diseased and pest-infested planting material is a serious issue. IITA has created many diseased-resistant cassava varieties,*

The general practice is that cassava should be planted at least two weeks before the beginning of the Rainy season and two weeks before the end of the Rainy season. There are several reasons for this, but the major reason for these planting recommendations are strictly based on our agricultural practices (rain-fed). The others are based on the nature of cassava and the pattern and nature of our rainfall which can be quite heavy compared to other parts of Africa and the world at large.

Planting 2 (two) to 3 (three) weeks before the beginning of the Rainy season will allow the plants to be settled before the heavy rains. The sporadic rains, during that brief period before the rainy season actually sets in, will provide enough moisture to maintain the plant for some time until they have gained hold of the soil. Regardless which method you use, if you plant just before or during heavy rains, the soil could very well be washed away and expose the cuttings.

Planting two weeks before the end of the Rainy season will also give the plants the necessary moisture they need. The reasons for this are obvious. The soil at this time should be full of moisture; and together with the last rainfalls, ***should*** provide the plants sufficient, water which should be able to sustain them through the dry season.

Remember, the cassava plant is very hardy and can thrive in almost every climatic condition, including drought conditions. So, the moisture that the plants will get during these periods ***should*** be enough to carry them through to maturity and up to harvest. Of course, the time you plant will be determined by your own climatic condition and weather pattern.

For us in Liberia and maybe, Sierra Leone and Guinea, we should be planting at the end of September or the beginning or middle of October; and sometime in March or April. I am beginning to get the idea that late January or mid-February might not be a bad time to plant. If you are prepared, planting after one of those heavy January or February rain showers might not be a bad idea.

However, if you want to play it safe, stick with the protocol and observe the weather pattern and decide what is best for you. Just remember *"Climate Change" and "Global Warming*" are real and have significant impacts on agriculture. The Rainy Season is supposed to end around October 15, the beginning of the Dry Season, but nowadays, the rains are extending into November and sometimes into December. And the Dry Season has no doubt become hotter, drier and to some degree, shorter. You must adjust your farming activities around these new realities. This is why we are stressing the word, "should".

More than one planting method can be used in the same field, but my recommendation is that you use one planting method. If you want to compare the various methods with their associated cost, time it takes to complete the process, and yields, then, you can plant smaller plots using different methods and measure the results. Again, just remember you have a nine to twelve months waiting period.

For me, I believe that cassava can be planted at any time of the year (except during the heavy rains), if you develop an adequate irrigation system. One thing to remember is that cassava does not need a lot water, and it does not like too much water either. However, I believe that with an efficient well-managed irrigation system, one can plant cassava in December and January and get a continuous supply of bountiful harvest. But that's a different topic for another time.

Words of Caution:

In Liberia, the Rainy Season is supposed to start at about April 15, and ends on October 15. That is the usual pattern. However, please be reminded that we have something now called, ***Climate Change.***

I believe that all of us are quite aware that in some cases the seasons are not only starting earlier or later (in some cases), but they are even lasting longer than usual; and the rains are heavier and the sun is hotter. So, please pay attention to the weather pattern and make the necessary adjustments. It is now raining up to mid December.

These words of caution do not only apply to Liberia. The also apply to other countries, especially Guinea (Conakry) and Sierra Leone, two countries that have similar rainfall patterns as Liberia. Climate change is real and affects the entire world; and the associated devastations is felt in every country and region. Therefore, not only should one be aware of this, but there is also a need to take the necessary precautions and make the adjustments in our farming practices.

Mechanized Cassava Planting Machines

Most of our discussions on planting cassava has been focused on manpower (human power), that is physical labour, even though, there were some mention of cassava planting equipment. In fact, in our part of the world, almost everything we do in agriculture, and what has have presented in this publication, from land preparation to planting and harvesting, involves physical labour. Why? This is simply how it is in our part of the world, and it is something, it seems, we cannot get away from. Even if we have the machines to do some of the work. Someone has to operate the equipment and someone has to repair it, if it breaks down. But that is something else compared to how we actually farm in Africa. If we really do want to improve agricultural productivity, improve the quality of the food we produce, and improve our economy in Liberia and elsewhere in Africa, mechanization is a must.

Of course, as was said earlier, what type of mechanization we need will depend on where we are in the agricultural process. There are mechanized solutions available in almost all aspect of agriculture production, especially, in the planting (sowing) and harvesting stages.

Most major cassava-producing countries like Brazil and the East Asian countries, like Thailand and China, employ mechanized cassava planters and harvesters. Up to the completion of this guide, I have not seen any in use in Liberia, but they are being used in some African countries like Nigeria, and Ghana. In fact, Kwame Nkrumah University of Science and Technology (KNUST) of Ghana (Kumasi) has developed an automated tractor-driven cassava harvester. These equipment make the job very easy. They can do in hours what it might take days to do. This cuts down the planting and harvesting time, improve productivity and save money. Remember, *"Time is money"*. Again, just remember you need the right size tractor.

Three varieties of tractor-drawn Cassava Planters, including a Power Tiller-driven version.

Mechanization is one of the reasons why we keep stressing "de-stumping", because these machine can only work effectively in a well-prepared fields that are fully de-stumped. Because, these cassava-planting and harvesting machines are either self-driven or tractor-driven, and they, in order to operate efficiently, must have little or no obstacles in their way.

Let me add that mechanization is not limited to machine-driven equipment. Animal-driven equipment can also be considered, to some extent, as mechanization. Unfortunately, for some reasons (perhaps cultural), they are not used in this part of the world. Almost every agricultural related activity here is human labour-driven, including transportation and land preparation. In my travels I have seen animal-powered equipment in use in other West African countries, including Burkina Faso, Ghana and Senegal; but not here in Liberia. In China and India, even with the availability of tractors, the use of animals to plough the land and transport agricultural goods is wide spread. Why? Perhaps, it is simply cultural practices; and that many farmers in these countries cannot afford to purchase a tractor or truck to do what these animals do. But for them it works, and I can assure you that many of the rice we consume from these countries are produced using some degree of animal power. Maybe, this is something that we need to think about and perhaps, develop a strategy that will train our farmers to do like wise.

Below are two photos, one from China and one from India, of animals being used to perform agriculture-related tasks. The photo on the left is that of oxen being used to plough the field. The one on the right is from India of a camel-driven transporter. Camels, horses, buffalos and oxen are widely used for these purposes in China and India. In my travels, I have, personally, also seen Donkeys and oxen being used in Burkina Faso and Ghana. And in Dakar (Senegal) horse-driven transporters are in regular use in the capital, Dakar.

Examples of Animal-Driven Mechanization

Photo on the Left is from China (Courtesy CATAS). Photo on the Left is from India (Taken by the author).

Crop Maintenance and Management

So, we have followed all the directions and our fields have been planted, and our crop is growing, hopefully, very well. So, what's next? Obviously, we must manage the field, making sure that crop maintenance and management chores, including weed control, fertilizer application (if necessary), and pest control are carried out to ensure that we have both quality and high yields. Pest control is a major crop maintenance activity. In this section, we will take a very close look at some of the pests that can cause damage to your cassava field and destroy your hard work. We did mention termites earlier, but there are other pests besides termites, which we need to be aware of. They are equally destructive and need to be controlled. However, before we do that, let us take a look at the two photos on the next page– Page 98.

The field in the top photo is well planted, even though, there are some opened spots. You can see that one could easily walk through it. This is what you want. A field that you can freely walk through. Overall, the field is well laid out. As you can see there are no stumps, and it would be very easy to managed and maintained.

The field in the bottom photo is quite different. It was planted using the old random-planting method. You can see how the field is tight and closed-in. You can also see how the weeds and other plant growth have taken over and have overshadowed the cassava plants. This is what you do not want. This situation, as is illustrated in the photo, can inhibit your plant growth and could be very difficult to managed. Cassava has difficulties not only competing effectively in this kind of environment, but trying to do a simple chore like weeding would be a major challenge.

Perhaps, the most important aspect of farming is the actual management of the field and the plants in it. Really, it actually boils down to what the professional agronomists call "Plant Protection". Protecting your farm and the crops growing in it from diseases, pests, weeds, thieves, animals and adverse weather, is serious business; and it demands your attention and time. This aspect of agriculture is so important that the government institution responsible for agriculture, the Ministry of Agriculture, has a whole department (Department of Plant Protection), dedicated to it. You should also place emphasis on protecting your plants.

One of the recommendations I will make is that you establish periodic visits to the field. Do not leave everything up to your farm manager, if you have one; or to your workers. Visit the field as often as possible and inspect the plants not just for weeds, insects, and diseases, but also to see how well they are growing. Do they need trimming? How are the stems growing? Are there dead spots or dead plants that need to be replaced? These are very important maintenance chores, that when done regularly, could improve yields and profitability. And remember your mangers need constant supervision. As the saying goes, Shine your eyes!"

This is an example of a well planted cassava field. See how the plants are spaced orderly?

A field planted the old random way. See, there is no order and the field is bushy and filled with weeds.

Take a look at the two photos above.

The top photo shows a field that was planted using the newer Flat/Horizontal method. The field was laid out and planted orderly. The bottom one shows a field planted the old random way. See the differences between the two fields? Which one of them do you think can be easily maintain?

Visiting the field regularly also allows you to be familiarized with the surroundings and the people in your employ and those living in nearby villages and towns. Let the people know who you are, and what you are trying to do. They could be your allies and act as your eyes and ears. They could also be destructive and a hindrance to your success. Handle them and your plants with the same love and care.

As you physically inspect the plants and walk through the field, my caution to you would be to be very careful and avoid compacting the soil and transmitting diseases to the plants. I would suggest that you get one of those white medical gowns or overcoats that doctors wear and put it on before walking through the plants. Perhaps, you could even wear rubber gloves. It is very important that you take extra precaution to protect your plants and your investment. Plants are living organisms just like us, and they are very sensitive and susceptible to catching diseases just as we are. Handle and protect them with care.

IDENTIFYING AND CONTROLLING CASSAVA DISEASES AND PESTS

Green Mite | Spider Mite | Mealybug | White Fly | *Dorysthenes granulosus* | Bull worm

Some of the bugs and insects that attack the cassava plant. (Photo is courtesy of CATAS)

Pest control is, and remains a major part of crop maintenance. It is very important for cassava farmers and producers to know that cassava, as with other plants, is susceptible to various insects, pests and diseases that affect its production and can destroy a lot of hard work and financial investments. Therefore, it is necessary that farmers or their managers (or both) are able to identify these insects and pests and have the necessary information, knowledge and technical skills on how to control and get rid of them.

In addition to these pests, cassava is also susceptible to various diseases and viruses including Cassava Mosaic Disease (CMD) and Cassava Root Rot Disease (CRRD), to name a few, which are prevalent in Africa. Many of our local (African) varieties are infested with CMD and CRRD, and the results can be from low yields to the loss of an entire field. These diseases and viruses are, in most cases, caused by pests and insects.

Unfortunately, most of our farmers and some of the local experts are not aware of these diseases or the pests that cause them, except, for a few who might have received some training from one of the various GOL and Donors-sponsored agriculture projects or from the NCSCC or CARI. Most cassava farmers know about termites and are quite aware of the destruction they can cause, and even though, they see some of these other insects, like the *Grasshopper, White Fly and Mealybug,* unfortunately, these farmers just do not have any idea how destructive these insects can be to their cassava plants, their entire field and their hard work.

This was confirmed by the ***Liberia Cassava Feasibility Study,***[50] commissioned by the NCSCC and conducted by IITA in collaboration with the MOA and CARI. In the Liberian study, farmers were shown these insects and the effects of the diseases and viruses on their cassava plants. And as was said above, they had no idea what they were; and neither did they know to what extent their crops were being affected by them. I highlight the NCSCC-IITA study because as Co-chairman of the NCSCC, I played some role in its implementation and validation. But more importantly, it is, perhaps, the most significant accomplishment of the NCSCC; and I believe that the study provides some

[50] *The Liberia Cassava Feasibility Study was commissioned by the NCSCC and conducted by IITA (2012). The exercise was lead by Dr. Richardson Okechukwu of IITA with support from the NCSCC and the MOA.*

Photos of Cassava Pests and Insects

Photo 1: Cassava mealy bug (Phenacoccus manicotti); Photo 2: White fly (Bemisia tabaci); Photo 3:Variegated grasshopper (Zonocerus variegatus); and Photo 4: Termites (Bugabug). (Photos courtesy of IITA Liberia Cassava Feasibility study.)

**All of the photos are courtesy of IITA: Liberia cassava Feasibility Study*

very important information that could be useful to all of us, especially, the farmer and producer.

The group of photos at the top of the page were taken by IITA researchers and published in the Liberian study. Take a close look at them. Can you see any similarities between the photos from CATAS (at the top of the previous page) and those at the top of this page? With a very close look, you will see that the insects in these two photos are basically the same, even though, one is from China and the other, from Africa. These insects are real, and they are widespread and exist everywhere cassava is grown.

The group of photos on the next page (103) shows the damages the pests and the viruses they create, can do to the cassava plant. Take a very good look at these photos. Have you seen any of these in the field? Perhaps not, if you are not a cassava farmer. If you are anywhere near where cassava is growing, take another look. You will see them because they are very prevalent. I am sure those of us who have some previous experience with cassava have seen them, but I am also very sure that we really ever thought anything much about it. Perhaps, we thought that this is the way cassava grows and simply , natural occurrences. No! They are not.

In any case, I hope that these photos help you to identify some of these pests, diseases, and viruses. My intention here is to make you aware that these diseases, viruses

Photos of some Cassava Diseases

Photo 1 & 2{ Cassava Mosaic Disease (CMD). Notice how the leaves are withered. Photo 3: Cassava Brown Leaf spots (CBLS). Photo 4: Cassava Bacterial Blight (CBB). Photo 5: Cassava Root Rot Disease (CRRD). Notice the rotted tuber. This normally caused by too much water. Photo 6: A Cassava plant infested with White Flies, one of the insects responsible for CMD.

**All photos are courtesy of IITA: Liberia cassava Feasibility Study, except for Photo 6, which was taken by the author.*

and pests do exist, so that when you do see some of them, you will know what they are. Hopefully, you will be able to take the necessary precautions and steps to avoid a bad situation, or try solve the problem before it get worse and destroys your investment. In most cases, there is not much you would be able to do about them at that time, but maybe, with the new knowledge and information, you can limit their occurrences in the future. The best way to control these diseases and prevent them from destroying your investment, is to avoid purchasing diseased planting material and introducing them into your field.

Additionally, if you do see them, it would also be good to alert the MOA and CARI. Most Ministries of Agriculture have a Department of Extension and Advisory Services with Extension Officers in the field who can also be alerted. In Liberia, the MOA has a County Agriculture Coordinator (CAC) and several District Agriculture Officers (DAO) in each of the 15 (fifteen) counties. These are extension officers from the MOA Department of Extension Services. They should be your first points of contact if you have any issues in the field or questions regarding the crop you are growing. At least, to my knowledge, this is how it is supposed to work. I am sure this is how it works in other countries in our region (ECOWAS) and elsewhere across Africa.

This is also good information to have, especially, when you are purchasing cassava cuttings or sticks. Perhaps, one of these Extension officers can be of assistance to you. In the case they cannot help you, they might be able to direct you to someone who might be able to provide the information you need. In fact, knowing who the extension officers are in your area of operation, or where your farm is located, is good not just for purchasing cassava cuttings. It is very important to know who the extension officers are because they can provide a lot of services to you, and most importantly, they can be your contact point with the Ministry of Agriculture and the community leaders in the area your farm is located. Believe me, extension officers can provide other services you might not even be aware of.

Having said this, it is very important and a must that you do everything possible to avoid buying diseased planting material. I suggest that when you are buying cuttings, you try to find out where they are coming from. If it is possible, you should do a thorough inspection of the field where they are coming from. That is, if you have the information. In addition, you should do everything possible to avoid buying cuttings without seeing where they come from. The last thing you want to do is to introduce infected planting material into your field. A CAC or DOA might know who the cassava farmers are and where they are located in their county and district of operation. Some of these farmers could be certified cassava growers trained by CARI, some NGO or one of the many MOA's donor-funded projects.

I really want you to have some idea of what you are dealing with. And perhaps, be able to control or limit the damage these pests and diseased planting material are capable of causing. Another precaution one should take in order to prevent these diseases and viruses from entering your field is to avoid bringing cassava cuttings from outside of the country. Believe it! It is not a good practice, not just for cassava, but also for other crops like Cocoa and Coffee. According to MOA technicians, this is how we got CMD in Liberia. It will not affect just your farm alone, but it can create problems for the entire country. BEWARE!

Honestly, many of us are guilty of this. We see a nice flower of plant in Nigeria or Kenya, and the next thing we do is pick it and put it in our luggage and bring it home. This is not a good practice, and we need to avoid it or stop it, if we are doing it.

Most of the work done at Cassava research institutions like CATAS, IITA and CARI is dedicated to eliminating these diseases and viruses. Controlling and eliminating the pests that are responsible for creating diseases and viruses like CMD and CRRD are the major focus of their work. Why? Because the main result of these diseases, viruses and pests are low yields and low quality of production, and they do have economic consequences. As a result, research institutions, including both CATAS and IITA spent quite a considerable amount of time and resources on creating new high-yielding and disease-free cassava varieties and developing strategies to control and eliminate these pests.

In West Africa, IITA (Ibadan, Nigeria) is the institution we deal with, even though, it has outstations in other parts of Africa and relationships with others institutions around the world, including CATAS.

Just for your information: it can take up to 10 (ten) years to develop a new disease-free or disease-resistant cassava variety. Once IITA creates a new high-yielding disease-resistant cassava or crop variety it is released and made available to the appropriate research institutions in Africa.

To get some of these new cassava varieties one will have to deal with their country's national research institutions, because IITA does not deal directly with individuals, as was said earlier. The way it works is, whether you are in Kenya, Nigeria, Liberia, Sierra Leone or Tanzania, IITA provides the government's research entity (in Liberia's case, CARI) with several newly-developed cassava varieties and the national research institution carries out field trials. The cassava scientists at these national research institutions conduct field tests and trials on them and select the ones they deem suitable for their respective country and propagate them. Eventually, they give them out to farmers (certified growers) who multiply them for onward distribution to other farmers and institutions in the country.

In Liberia's case, CARI has over the last few years received more than 200 cassava varieties from IITA; and so far, as I am aware, they have released 8 (eight) different varieties (including the *TME 419 and Yellow Root*) to the public. Most of us just refer to the TME 419 as the "four-one-nine" variety. Honestly, I cannot tell you what these released-varieties are. Some of these varieties are listed in the table in *Appendix 4* on page 147-148.

There is detailed list of pests and diseases in a report I wrote and published on the training provided by CATAS for African countries: ***A Report on the Training Course on Cassava Production and Processing Technology for African Countries (July 25-August 16, 2012).***

In the report, I go into much more detail on Cassava Pest and diseases. I really do not want to repeat it here. The scope of this guide is limited, and it is not intended to delve into the complex issue of cassava diseases and pests and their control. In that report, I looked at the 16 (sixteen) cassava diseases, which CATAS has identified, in detail. In this guide, I only want to deal with the ones identified in the Liberian study conducted by IITA and the NCSCC with support from CARI. I believe that it should be the responsibility of the MOA, CARI, and the NCSCC to provide this information to farmers. The NCSCC was created by the Liberian government through the National Cassava Strategy to develop, manage and promote the development of the Liberian Cassava industry in concert with the MOA and other related government ministries, agencies with farmers, cooperatives, trade associations, the private sector and donors.

I don't want to spend too much time on this, even though, this is very important information to have. If you are interested in more information on this, I suggest that you contact your national research institute (CARI in Liberia), or get a copy of the ***Liberia Cassava Feasibility Study*** (Dr. Richardson Okechukwu, IITA, 2011), or ***A Report on the Training Course on Cassava Production and Processing Technology for African Countries*** (H. Augustus Roberts, Jr. (2012).

Controlling Termites

The termite is another pest which should also be controlled and managed in your plant maintenance program. However, in the case of termites, they ought to be dealt with at the land selection, land preparation and planting stages in addition to the plant maintenance stage. The termite, ("bugabug" as we call it in Liberia) is one of those pests that can wreak serious havoc on your project. Therefore, it is absolutely important that you try to deal with them at the first two stages of your project, land selection and land preparation. And then, at the planting stage as mentioned above. They must be identified and every effort must be made to control or eliminate them.

Termites at work.

As was said earlier, farmers traditionally use 3-4 cuttings when they plant. The termite is one of the main reasons why farmers do this. Their rationale has always been, and still is, that they might lose a few cassava sticks (cuttings/stems) to termites, but the rest will grow. This is very true. Termites are a major concern. That is why they should be dealt with at all cost. If you can avoid them, please do. If not, then you must take steps to get rid of them or try limitting the damage that they are capable of causing. They can cause serious damage to your crop and affect your investment. This is very important, and it cannot be stressed enough; and I might add, *"it easier said than done"* as the saying goes.

There are very few things one can do without resulting to heavy pesticide use. The best way to control termites is to do all you can to avoid them as much as possible. I know that this does not provide any real solution, but it only illustrates the challenges

More Challenges:

This piece of land has been cut, slashed, burned, and is being readied for planting. Notice the termite hills in the background. There are four of them. (See the arrows.) This could be big trouble for the farmer in the future. This is where one should start looking for a solution to deal with the prevailing situation before planting the crop.

associated with dealing with these hardy insects. I would suggest that you consult the technical experts at the Ministry of Agriculture, your research institute (for Liberia, CARI) or perhaps, the EPA (Environmental Protection Agency) for advice. In fact, the local farmers might be able to help. A word to the wise is quite sufficient.

One the biggest challenges to termite control is getting rid of the queen. If you can find a way to do that, then you are good to go. These termites are resilient, and under the leadership of the "queen" they are capable of regrouping before you know it. Even if you use a tractor or bull dozer to break down the termite hills, they will eventually come back and regroup once the queen is alive. She will always regroup her troops. Farmers do have some strategies that they use. So, please consult them. With this information we can move on.

Before we move on, let us take a look at the photo at the bottom of the previous page (107). The photo is an illustration of a typical termite-infested piece of farmland. Notice that it has been cut, slashed and burnt, but yet the termite hills are prominent. What do you do in this situation? This is where some of the major challenges are in agriculture. You, as a farmer, cannot ignore this situation. It might cost you more than you had imagine at the beginning of your land preparation exercise, but you have to deal with it then, or it might cost you more in the future.

Controlling Weeds

As was stated earlier, cassava is a weak competitor to weeds, and its growth and the quality of its yield are seriously reduced and compromised by weed competition. Therefore, weeding is not only an important component of cassava field management and maintenance, but it also has several benefits to the cassava crop if done properly. There are some recommendations which will be provided as a guide for controlling weeds, but before we provide those recommendations. Let us take a more detailed look at the issue of "weed control".

Even though, controlling weed growth in cassava production is important, it must also be noted that this is not only limited to cassava. Controlling weed growth in the field is an important crop maintenance activity for every crop you grow. So, it is very important that you have the right information, and that you use it properly. We do not have to wait to start weed control exercises after we plant. The process of controlling and preventing weed overgrowth among our crops, whatever they are, can be initiated before planting and right after planting. However, we must be very cautious in our approach and be careful what we use and how we use it.

Most weed-control activities are labor-intensive. You have to physically get into the field using the right equipment in addition to just rolling up your sleeves and getting down on your hands and knees, getting dirty, to pull out the weeds.

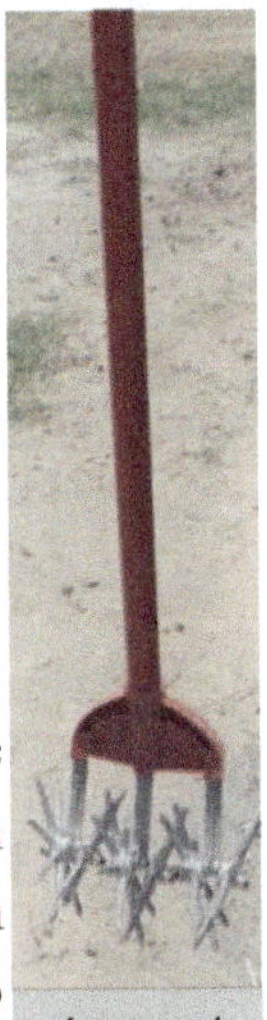
A manual mechanical Weedier

Weed control can also be done with herbicides or mechanical devices. In very large cassava production, the cassava field can be sprayed with herbicides before planting. In Brazil, they use these large industrial sprayers attached to a tractor and spray dozens of hectares of a cassava field before planting the cassava using tractor-drawn cassava planters. The photo on the right is an example of a handheld mechanical weedier.

If you use herbicides in your project, you must take all the necessary precautions and make sure that the product you use is safe and legally acceptable and approved by the authorities to use. Herbicides are effective, but they can have serious environmental consequences, if they are not applied properly. In addition, there are many herbicides which have been banned and are illegal to use. A list of banned agrochemicals is available in the appendix. If you do use a herbicide, please make sure that it is legal to use and environmentally-friendly. And please do everything to follow the manufacturer's instruction on how to use it.

The EPA does not only have a department that can advise you, but it also works and collaborates with the MOA and other agencies and laboratories, nationally and regionally, to ensure that the right and legally acceptable herbicides are used. In addition to having a list of banned and illegal agrochemicals which you can consult, the EPA has its own laboratory and list of EPA-accredited laboratories that you can consult. The list of accredited labs are listed in the appendix.

Herbicides are a subset of agrochemicals. So, my final advice is that you be very careful using herbicides or any agrochemicals, including fertilizers that fit in this category. Why? Your customers, the consumers of your product are the main reasons. They can make or break your business. Nowadays, consumers are more informed and quite concerned about what goes into their bodies and how the environment is affected by our agricultural practices. Be very careful that your business is not affected by how you grow your product.

If you do use herbicides or other agrichemicals, please provide the information on your product's label. There is something called "traceability". And there is also "accountability". It is better for your consumers or buyers to know what they are getting, rather than them finding out through some third-party tests after purchase. Remember, some of these chemicals are allowable in certain quantities. Once they meet those requirements, there should not be any problems. You will only have a problem when those allowable quantities are exceeded. Please do the research, get the proper and legally accepted product and follow the instructions on how to apply them.

This is where traceability and accountably come in. Not only that you must be held accountable when something is discovered in your product, you must also be able to trace its origins. Where in your production cycle did it enter?

As I said, the EPA has its own laboratory and a list of EPA-accredited laboratories. I, personally, visited the EPA facility. I was very impressed with the information that was provided to me and the professionalism exhibited by the person in charge. I would suggest that you visit your environmental regulatory agency also. I was quite surprised when I visited the EPA. I did not know that they had their own laboratory facilities. It is not a very large facility, but it could be very useful.

The information and recommendations below are from our study at CATAS and is based on extensive research by both IITA and CATAS.

- Weeding loosens the soil and benefit the formation of larger roots, creates resistant to drought and keep moisture which results to higher yields.
- Cassava fields need to be weeded at least 2-3 times during the crop cycle, usually at 1, 2 and 3 months after planting.
- Weeding can be controlled by 3 means: labor, herbicide and mechanically.
    - ⇒ Labor weeding should be done as follows:
        - ◊ First weeding: 1 month after planting. (Fertilizer could also be applied at this time.)
        - ◊ Second weeding: 2-3 months after planting.
        - ◊ More weeding can be done according to condition.

- ⇒ Herbicide Weeding offers the following benefits:
    - ◊ Provides very good results
    - ◊ Uses less labor
    - ◊ Helps to maintain moisture
    - ◊ Reduces soil and water erosion,
    - ◊ Increases yield and income

*Please note the following:

- ⇒ When using herbicide to control weeds, care should be taken to avoid spraying herbicide on young seedlings, green stems, buds and leaves.
- ⇒ Mechanized Weeding is extremely effective and employs very little human labor; however, equipment can be expensive and in most cases are not readily available.

Weeds can also be controlled naturally by intercropping other crops, utilizing the cassava own growth pattern.

- ♦ Intercropping:
    - ⇒ Intercropping with certain crops (groundnuts, watermelon, pumpkin, rice) is another option for controlling weeds, and it can reduce the physical work significantly. How does it work? Because of the way these crops grow, they provide a covering around the cassava plant. This suppresses the weed and prevents it from growing.
- The Cassava Growth pattern
    - ⇒ The cassava's own growth pattern can also help in controlling weed growth. I know it sounds repetitive, but we encourage you to use one of the newer planting methods because they play a very big role in controlling weed growth with the cassava own growth pattern. Once you use one of these methods, the Cassava makes it very easy to control weeds by the way it grows. After about six weeks, the cassava leaves create a canopy. This effectively blocks the sunlight from reaching the ground, and thus limits weeds' growth which need sunlight as all other plants, to grow and develop.

Fertilizers Use

The application of fertilizers is a part of crop maintenance and management and should be included in your crop's maintenance and management program. The recommendations on the use of fertilizers on cassava is based primarily on training and recommendations received from CATAS and the results of CATAS' 12-year research on fertilizer use on Cassava through the Chinese Tropical Crops Genetic Resource Institute (TCGRI).[51] Even though, the CATAS cassava training program for African countries was several years ago, the recommendations are still very valid.

In addition to the recommendations from CATAS, IITA, in collaboration with the National Root Crops Research Institute (Nigeria) has also developed a very detailed fertilizer-use protocol, *Tailored Fertilizer Application Recommendations for Cassava.*[52] The recommendations are not very different from those recommended by CATAS, but it is very detailed. It is available as a leaflet on IITA's website. Much of what will be presented here will be information from both of these institutions.

Let me also add that CATAS has developed extensive working relationships with IITA and several African countries' Ministries of Agriculture, including the DRC (Democratic Republic of the Congo), Nigeria and Sierra Leone. In addition, some operatives from the MOA (Liberia) have had advanced trainings at CATAS, including, post-graduate studies.

Before we get into the issue of fertilizer usage, it is very important to understand what fertilizers are, and why do we need them, especially, since we believe that the African soil is so good that anything can grow in it. In fact, in Liberia, we have this notion that all we have to do is dig a hole, put a seed in it; and "voila" it will grow. Some people believe that you do not even have to dig a hole, just throw the seed on the ground, and it will sprout. But this is not entirely true. We discussed this earlier, so, it is not necessary to go back there.

According to IITA, cassava requires different nutrients to grow, and the 3 (three) most important nutrients are Nitrogen (N), Phosphorous (P) and Potassium (K)- NPK. Now you know where *"NPK"* come from. It is the combination of these 3 nutrients. So, lets take a look a them individually and see what exactly they do and provide for your cassava.

1. Nitrogen (N): Nitrogen is required for the growth of the cassava stem and leaves.
2. Phosphorous (P): this nutrient is necessary and provides the energy that the

51 TCGRI- The Tropical Crops Genetic Resource Institute is a research institute of the Chinese Academy of Tropical Agriculture Sciences (CATAS) was established in 1958 and located in Hanain, China.

52 Tailored Fertilizer Application Recommendations for Cassava, published by IITA. For more information visit www.acai-project.org or contact s.adekunbi@cgiar.org.

plant needs to grow adequately.
3. Potassium (K): potassium is the nutrient that plant need to develop the roots adequately.

Now that you have the information, you can tailor your fertilizer application to which value-added cassava product you want to produce and market. If you want to produce and market cassava leaves or cassava sticks, you know that you need nitrogen. Having said this, please do not go and overuse nitrogen. Remember that cassava needs all three of these nutrients to grow adequately, but the amounts you use depends on the "fertility of the soil and the time (date) we plant.[53]

*Remember our discussion on 'soil-testing?' See the importance now?

Based on the information provided, the following recommendations are offered. They are based on both TGCRI and IITA recommendations:

- Before applying fertilizer, you must first establish that there is a problem. In other words, why does the plant need fertilizer in the first place? Will the application of fertilizer help solve the problem?
- Fertilization is not recommended on new land or in the first planting season.
- What was the yield you got in the past planting season without fertilizer use?
- Limit the use of fertilizer in fertile land. (Based on soil tests results.)
- More fertilizer should be considered in less fertile land. (Based on soil tests results.)
- First fertilization should be carried out 1 month after planting using the following combination:
    - ⇒ ***150 kg urea and 150-200 kg KCL, mix 150-300 kg compound fertilizer and apply.***[54]
- Second fertilization should be applied 3-4 months after planting.

The *Tailored Fertilizer Application Recommendations for Cassava* flyer published by IITA provides the following 6 steps for fertilizer application to cassava:

Step 1: Apply Good Agronomic Practices.

- Prepare, layout and plant the field as recommended using improved diseased-free/tolerant varieties if available

Step 2: Choose the best fertilizer.
Step 3: Decide the Fertilizer application rate.

---

[53] *From "Tailored Fertilizer Application Recommendations for Cassava", published by IITA. For more information visit www.acai-project.org or contact s.adekunbi@cgiar.org.*

[54] *This is a fertilizer combination recommended by CATAS.*

Step 4: Calculate the Costs and Benefits of using fertilizer.

Step 5: Apply fertilizer at the right time.

Step 6. Apply fertilizer the right way.

We are not going into the details of all of the 6 steps. The flyer is available, and we have provided the link. However, it would be good to take a closer look at Steps 3, 4 and 5.

Step 3: Decide the Fertilizer application rate.

The rate at which fertilizer should be used is based on what your yields were in the past without fertilizer use. Remember that fertilizer is not recommended in your first planting season.

These are the guidelines as follows:

⇒ If your yield was less than 15 tons per hectare, Apply Fertilizer.
⇒ If your yield was the same, between 15 and 20 T per hectare. You can use fertilizer, if you are willing to take the risk. If not, do not apply fertilizer.
⇒ If your yield is higher than 20 T/ha, do not apply fertilizer.
⇒ Below is a formula provided by IITA to calculate fertilizer needed in a given planted area. It is based on the generally accepted rule that 1 bag (50 kg) of fertilizer is required for 1 ha.

Here is the formula (from the IITA website):

$$\frac{\text{Area of your field } (m^2) \times \text{Fertilizer needed for 1 ha (kg)}}{10{,}000\ (m^2)} = \text{Fertilizer needed for your field your}$$

Basically, it is very easy to see that each hectare requires 1 (one) 50 kg-bag of fertilizer. But what if we had something less or more or not exactly even. The formula provides a solution.

*Based on this calculation, *1 bag of 50 kg fertilizer is equal approximately to 1 (one full bottle cap of fertilizer per plant.*

Step 4: Calculate the Costs and Benefits.

IITA advises that fertilizer use only makes sense if the value of the projected yield is larger than the cost of the fertilizer. Therefore, you must calculate the benefits of higher yields based on what cassava is selling for.

Step 5: Apply fertilizer at the right time.

Whatever you do, remember that it is very important that fertilizers are applied at the right time and in the right way. Please refer to the recommendations as listed above. IITA also recommends that fertilizer is applied when the soil is moist and after 1 (one) or 2 (two) rain showers.

*It must be noted here that fertilizer use is not necessary, and therefore, not a must, especially in the first year of planting.

Types of Fertilizers

Basically, there are two types of fertilizers: Organic and Chemical. Organic fertilizers can be further divided into Animal Manure and Green Manure. Our recommendation here, as it relates to fertilizer usage, is that one should be very careful in the use of chemical fertilizers, and they should be used only after thorough research and based on your own requirements and needs, and targeted customers' requirement. These are very important considerations, and one must be very cautious when using chemical fertilizers.

The major concerns are related to health and food safety issues, because these fertilizers, whether chemical or organic, will eventually find their way into our food systems and finally into our bodies. The other reason is economic, especially, if we want to export our produce. We must be aware that many countries, particularly, the European Union (EU) countries, do not want to import chemical-laden foods into their countries.

This is the reality. So, think about it before applying these fertilizers and agrochemicals. If you do use fertilizers or agrochemicals do not conceal it. I would suggest that you list whatever fertilizers or chemicals you use on your produce's labels. This is transparency, integrity and an honest way of doing business. It would not be good if your customers were to find out this information on their own. It could destroy your business.

There is a third reason, the environment. Yes, fertilizers and agrochemicals do have impact on our environment, and therefore, we should be aware of the damage they can do to the environment and our health. Remember, "Climate change is real and affects every aspect of our lives."

In fact, quite recently, the EU has come up with a new set of regulations, that should come into effect on December 31, 2024, which restricts the importation of products into the EU which are grown from deforested areas. The regulations, referred to as the EUDR: New Regulation on Deforestation-Free Chocolate Products,[55] are quite restric-

[55] *The EUDR - Regulation (EU) 2023/1115 on deforestation-free products mandates that any operator or trader dealing with commodities like cocoa must ensure their products are not sourced from recently deforested land or contribute to forest degradation.*

tive, detailed and voluminous for me go into here. The regulations cover several issues, including traceability, human rights and the use of fertilizers and agrochemicals. Even though this particular regulation focuses on Cocoa, it could be expanded and applied to other produce. Therefore, one must be aware of these types of trade policies, which I believe might be adopted by other regions, including the African Union as it implements the Africa Continental Free Trade Area (AfCFTA). Additionally, the post-Malabo Agenda, the Kampala Declaration,[56] which is the third generation CAADP, focuses on the development of a holistic sustainable African Food Systems that is not only sustainable but also incorporates *Smart Agriculture.* Once again, Climate Change is real and all of us have to do our part to control and limit its effects.

In addition, cassava is notorious for depleting the nutrients in the soil. Therefore, based on the information provided, there is a need for some type of intervention. However, we should be very careful when applying fertilizers. You should get as much information as possible and look at alternative strategies before rushing in with fertilizers, most especially with chemical fertilizers. The recommendations from IITA, CATAS and other research institutions must be taken seriously and followed. In addition, intercropping with groundnuts can accomplish some of what you might want with fertilizers. It should also be considered.

The same caution should be taken with agrochemicals use. Please do the research and get the proper information. Most of the diseases that affect cassava are from viruses and agrochemicals, in most cases, will not, and do not work. However, if you going to consider fertilizer and agrochemical use, for other aspects of pest management, please follow the guidelines that have been provided and read the instructions from the manufacturer that come with the material that you purchase.

Alternatives and other Fertilization Strategies

In addition to the traditional chemically manufactured fertilizers, there are other strategies and alternatives which could be very effective instead of relying wholly on manufactured fertilizers, which could be very expensive, especially for smallholder farmers. In this section, we will take a brief look at some of these alternatives and strategies, which, in many cases, are quite effective, environmentally friendly and very affordable. These alternatives are basically organic. Before we discuss these alternatives or any fertilizer use, it is very important that you be reminded that before you apply any fertilizer, you must find out if there is really a need for fertilizer application in the first place. This was mentioned earlier.

Secondly, it is just as important to find out which nutrients are missing from your soil

56 *The post-Malabo Agenda, the Kampala Declaration will be formally adopted and launched by the AUC in January 2025 at Kampala, Uganda.*

and which nutrients you really need for the particular crop. In this case for cassava. For the second consideration, unfortunately, the issue is whether you can afford to conduct the appropriate soil tests. As was established earlier, the information from the soil test should guide you in your fertilizer application processes.

For cassava, one good strategy that you could use is: after your first harvest, instead of replanting cassava, plant the field with groundnuts (peanuts). How would that work? Let us say that you have a very large parcel of land (about 5-10 hectares), but you only planted about a hectare or two in the first year with cassava. In the second year, you can develop a strategy where, instead of replanting cassava after harvesting the cassava, plant groundnuts in the old harvested-field and cassava in the newer portions of the land.

The theory is that the groundnuts will replenish the soil with needed nutrients which the cassava might have depleted. Since groundnut is a short-term crop, you might be able to replant that portion of the land with cassava before the cassava-planting season is over after you harvest the groundnuts. Remember groundnuts have major economic value also; and it could also help finance your project. So, technically, this strategy could provide two benefits- fertilization and financial.

In addition to this, there are other strategies or alternatives which could be considered. For this guide, I would like for us to look at two strategies which are not only effective and environmentally friendly but could also provide some degree of sustainability and economic benefit to your project or business.

Strategy 1: Compost production; creating your own organic fertilizer

Composting is defined as, "The natural process of recycling organic matter, such as leaves and food scraps, into a valuable fertilizer that can enrich soil and plants. Anything that grows decomposes eventually; composting simply speeds up the process by providing an ideal environment for bacteria, fungi, and other decomposing organisms (such as worms, sow bugs, and nematodes) to do their work. The resulting decomposed matter, which often ends up looking like fertile garden soil, is called compost. Fondly referred to by farmers as "black gold," compost is rich in nutrients and can be used for gardening, horticulture, and agriculture."[57]

This old wooden box is perfect for composting.

Honestly, I cannot say anymore than this and neither can I add anything to the definition, because this definition provided by NRDC (the National Resource Defense Council) is not only clear,

[57] *Composting 101 from NRDC - https//www.nrdc.org/stories/composting101#whatis by Sheila Hu*

but tells us, exactly, what compost is composed of, what it looks like, what is used for, and how it is created. Even with this information, there is a need to go into some details in order to guide you as you attempt to create your own compost.

Compost development or creation is not difficult. It is a very simple process and the tools and materials you need are readily available. The two most important materials you need are the organic materials (leaves, food wastes or leftovers, rotted vegetables and fruits, peelings, etc.) and something in which to store the materials. The Storage container could be a small (or large) barrel, a wooden box, a small plastic container, a pit or concrete enclosure. The size of your storage container will be dependent on the size of your project and your fertilizer needs.

I developed a small compost system for my household plants using a used plastic garbage container in which I deposited all the leftovers food stuff from my house, including fish, meat bones, fruits and other plant materials. Periodically, I added soil and constantly turned it over. It worked very well for me and my plants. If you have a small farm or a medium size project, you will have to invest a bit more, especially in your storage facility. Of course, a larger project will require a larger storage facility.

The major challenge for a large composting system is getting the organic material you will need. This could also be a challenge for small projects. The issue is where to get the material from, because it is obvious that leftovers from your home will not be sufficient. This is where you have to be creative and spend some money. So, where do you get the organic material from? The markets where foodstuff, vegetables and fruits are sold and restaurants are the best sources for organic materials. Even if you get the material free you will still have to transport it to your site, and that involves spending money. But it is money that would be well-spent and worth its weight in gold, "black gold" that is.

In Liberia, composting is being successfully implemented by a women-led farmer based organization (FBO), Women in Agriculture for Sustainable Development (WASUDEV). WASUDEV is headed by a farmer, entrepreneur, and community activist, Ms. Hawa Dunor-Varney, the CEO. The group's entire farming activity and productive system is organic. Because their farm is a bit large, they dug a pit to store and process their compost. It is in this pit that they deposit all of the organic material to create the compost. The compost from the pit is distributed throughout the farming area at the time of planting. Composting is an integral part of their farming practices.

Now the question is how does one know when the composting material is ready? Usually, when you start seeing earthworms in the soil, your compost is ready.

Using compost in agricultural practices

In the Photo on the left women farmers are transferring compost to the field for use. In the photo on the right farmers are planting seeds in compost-filled holes. As you can see this can also be done with cassava. (Photos, courtesy of WASUDEV.

The two photos at the top of the page are from WASUDEV. In the photo on the left, the compost produced by the group is being transferred to the planting area where farmworkers, in the picture on the right are placing seeds in the compost in pre-dug holes where seeds will be planted. As you can see, this process can also be applied to cassava, even though I do have some reservations on the amount of compost that is being placed in the holes.

What is important here and the major takeaway, is that composting could be an excellent alternative to manufactured or chemical fertilizers. However, as with manufactured fertilizers, compost should also be used in a manner that it not only provides the nutrients that your crops need, but it should be used economically and efficiently. In other words, do not overkill its usage just because it is organic. Overuse of fertilizers, regardless which type it is, is one of the major concerns of agronomists and extension providers, globally. Many farmers ignore the manufacturer's recommendations and instructions and apply too much or too little fertilizers that, in the end, the fertilizer provides no real benefits to the crop. So, whether it is organic or manufactured fertilizer, follow the instructions and recommendations; and in some cases, just experiment with smaller plots and see what works best.

Besides its apparent benefits to your crops, there are two other benefits to composting, environmental and financial; and these should be seriously considered as you develop your composting strategy. Composting is very important to the environment because it provides an excellent waste management strategy, not only for household waste but also for farm waste.

Composting could also increase the economic value of your project in more ways than one. First, composting can be a source of additional income for you from selling excess compost to other farmers. Not only can you sell compost, but you could also provide training to farmers for a fee; or you can develop an arrangement where you can purchase their (farmers you train) excess compost for your personal use or sale.

Additionally, composting could increase the economic value of your project. Not only could you sell your extra compost, as was mentioned above, but you could also use it as a marketing tool.

The second economic value that you could enjoy from composting is from the way your business is marketed and viewed by consumers and the public, in general. You could market your business as an *"Environmental Sensitive"* or *"Environmental Friendly"* business. This should add value to your business. Why? With the global awareness and issues of *Climate Change, Global Warming* coupled with environmental degradation, consumers are more aware and sensitive to how the food they eat is produced and how farming practices affect the environment. Having your business labelled or marketed as *"Sustainable Agriculture," "Organic," or "Environmentally Sensitive"* will add value to the products you produce and hence, your business.

Strategy 2: System of Rice Intensification

Another strategy that you could use is the pre-application of fertilizer to the field. This is a fertilization strategy used in the System of Rice Intensification (SRI).[58] SRI is a rice production technique which was introduced to Liberian rice farmers several years ago through a training program sponsored by WAAP, FARA and in collaboration with CHAP. It is not necessary to go into all the details here because SRI involves many processes. However, there is one aspect of the SRI that I believe can be adapted and used in cassava production. That is, the way the field is prepared before planting. In fact, SRI has evolved into the SCI (System of Crop Intensification) because some aspect of it has been successfully adapted and employed in the production of other crops. Therefore, I believe that it can also be applied to cassava production.

Before introducing this system to you, the cassava grower, you must first have an idea of how rice is traditionally grown. Rice is a crop that needs a lot of water and normally, its seeds are broadcast in the field. Most rice in Liberia are grown upland, even though there is a significant move to grow rice in the lowlands. In the SRI, rice is not grown in the traditional way. It is grown in a more orderly manner as cassava is grown now.

In SRI, instead of broadcasting rice seeds, the seeds are first placed in nurseries and then the rice seedlings are transplanted to a water-flooded field where they are planted, in an orderly manner with a predefined plant spacing just as cassava is planted in the new planting methods. The difference is the flooded field, and how it is prepared. As we already know, cassava does not like a whole lot of water. So then, why are we talking about SRI and cassava? According to the available data from CHAP, SRI uses less

58 *SRI : System of Rice Intensification is a non-traditional rice production technology,*

seeds and produces higher yields,[59] just as cassava produced by one of the newer planting methods are more productive.

For Cassava production, we only want to consider the fertilizer application technique used in SRI. In SRI, organic fertilizer is spread and distributed into the plot or growing area of the rice prior to planting the rice seedlings. SRI does not use chemical fertilizer, instead it uses organic fertilizers, mostly animal manure. So, by the time the rice seedlings are planted, the soil would have been fully fertilized. This is simple and there is no need to get into any technical discussion here. The main challenge would be acquiring the quantity of manure or organic material you might need. This is where you have to be innovative and "think out of the box". You can either make your own organic material as was illustrated in the previous strategy; or you can contact livestock breeders or the people who sell cattle. For Liberia. if you live near or have access to Monrovia, you can contact the National Slaughter House which is located on Somalia Drive on Bushrod Island. There is a lot of manure available there. You can get it practically free of charge. The only consideration will be the cost of transportation.

Finally, as we consider fertilizer use in our cassava production, and perhaps other crops, we might decide to produce and the alternative strategies which have been recommended in this guide, there are other strategies, we did not discuss. My intent was not to go into the subject with any real detail because as was already said, fertilizer application in cassava production, especially, in its first of production is not recommended. But that does not mean you cannot apply it the future. However, I thought it was important to give some basic information that would help guide you as consider increasing your yield and quality of production. I hope I have done that.

In addition to this, it is important to note that the EUDR regulations and the sustainable African Food System are not the only considerations when contemplating fertilizer use. There are the 10 principles of RAI which was mentioned earlier and the United Nations SDGs (Sustainable Development Goals), particularly, those with links to agricultural production (SDGs 2, 9,12, & 13), which are, unfortunately, beyond the scope of this guide; but they must also be considered in your work. Please do the research.

IMPORTANT WORDS OF CAUTION ON THE USE OF FERTILIZERS:

Everything about agriculture is based on quality and quantity. Quality and quantity are very important measurements of economic value to a farmer's field and to his or her hard work. Sometimes our desire for quality and quantity leads us to the use of fertilizers and agrochemicals without careful research and proper guidance. We must be very careful in this regard. Contrary to popular belief, the Liberian soil is not as great as we think it is. This is the conclusion that all of the experts and soil scientists have reached, including the experts at FAO and the MOA. So, there is a need for some interventions to help boost our productive capacity. In addition, there are many African scientists and researchers who do not believe that we (African) can achieve food security or sovereignty without the use of fertilizers. However, we must be very careful how we intervene. As was said earlier, many consumers have become quite concerned about ingesting fertilizers and agrochemicals.

[59] *SRI is 8kg per ha, and minimum yield currently per ha is 4 tons with an average productive tiller of 45. Seedlings are transplanted from 8 days to 15 days at 2 to 3 leaves and plant per hill. Traditionally it is 25 kg per ha and 1.5 tons per ha yields. (CHAP)*

INTERCROPPING

Intercropping, as was stated earlier, can be used as a strategy to control weeds, but it is even more important than just a weed-controlling strategy. Intercropping can provide some very important economic benefits to farmers and it should be used for both purposes: *weed-control and economics*. To be honest this is a topic that could have been discussed at the planting stage, but as was said earlier, it would be good to read the guide before we start our project. As important and valuable as *"intercropping"* might be, many farmers might not bother to intercrop, especially, large-scale farmers. But the benefits it can provide to small-scale farmers compels its discussion. In fact, farmers do intercrop, but are they doing it right? That is why this section is very important.

The thing to remember here is, that most cassava varieties, except a few, take a long time (9-12 months) to mature. So, while one is waiting for it to fully mature, what should one do? Farmers, being the smart people they are, understand this very well. It is one of the major reasons why our (African) farmers are multi-crop-farmers, especially, cassava farmers. They just cannot afford to wait for 9-12 months for the cassava to mature before they start consuming it and earning some income from it. So, they plant other shorter life-cycle crops in addition to their cassava and rice. You should also. But the question is, "How should the farmer go about it? Develop a separate planting area for the other crops?" No! Not necessarily. The farmer can use the same area that was prepared and laid out for the cassava or rice and plant the other crop among the primary crop. Simply put, that is what is called "intercropping".

This is one of the added advantages of intercropping. The farmer or you, for instance, do not have to develop a separate field for the other crops that could be planted within

A typical intercropped-cassava field. This field is intercropped with Corn.

and amongst the cassava. Rather than you developing and preparing separate fields for the other crops, you can use that same field which has already been laid out and properly prepared.

A word of caution, please be aware that not every crop can be intercropped with cassava or rice for that matter. What we do know is that corn (maize), sweet potatoes, groundnuts, watermelon, pumpkin, rice, and soybeans are excellent for intercropping with cassava. Perhaps the six-week Okra might also work, but I have not tried it, and there is no information to support this. So, I cannot guarantee that it (the okra) will work. But it is worth trying.

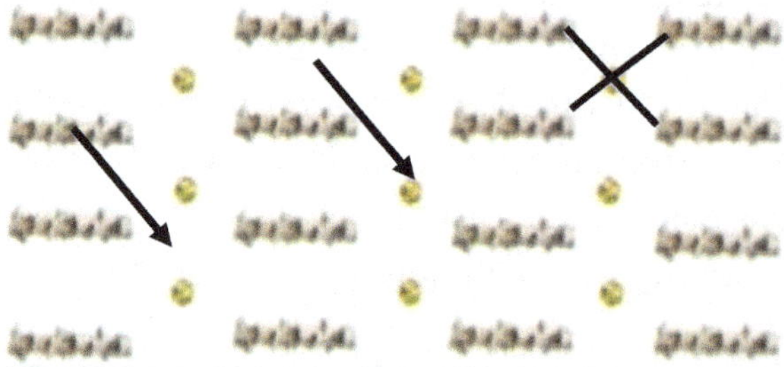

What you can do is plant a smaller plot and experiment? But if you are going to try intercropping with Okra, you cannot broadcast the Okra seeds among the cassava, you must plant the okra orderly as the cassava is planted. (Please see the illustration below.) The results, if they are good, can then be used in the future and tried with larger plots. Do not be afraid to experiment.

Experimenting with different crops will allow you see what works best. If you do experiment, we suggest that you try plants that take six weeks (maximum) to mature and harvest. Why? Because it is at about that time that the cassava should have created its canopy, and we do not want any activities within the plants that would disturb or damage the plants. This also applies to weeding activities. They can also disturb the cassava plants. If you do not want to experiment, intercrop with the recommended crops. Intercropping with these crops provides excellent weed control also. In the case of groundnuts, they do provide some fertilization by putting some nutrients back into the soil.

Intercropped Cassava-Planted Field

Cassava can also be intercropped with some long-term crops like, cocoa, oil palm, rubber and fruit trees. The benefits are both short and long-termed. The Cassava can provide the same economic benefits to these long-term crops as the short-term crops provide to the cassava. While you are waiting for your Rubber, Cocoa or Oil Palm to grow, which can take from two to five years, depending on the variety of the particular long-term crop, the cassava can help recoup some of your investment. There are newer varieties of Oil Palm, and Cocoa that start producing in two to three years compared to the older varieties.

*Please note that CATAS does not recommend Rubber for intercropping with Cassava in Africa and the Americas because of the issue of diseases. Rubber is a close relative of cassava and both crops share similar diseases.[60] At the time, the Chinese were trying to build a rubber industry, and they were very concerned that planting cassava in close proximity to rubber trees would, eventually, affect their rubber plants.

I strongly recommend that as you plan your cassava project, you take a serious look at intercropping. However, as beneficial as intercropping might be, you have to take into consideration that the cassava plant is not very competitive with other crops, and therefore, intercropping could affect its yield and that of the other crop also, if not done properly. In fact, yields will always be affected, even if it done properly, but benefits could well cancel out the negatives. You will have to experiment with different crops and see which one will not have an adverse affect on your cassava plant and which ones are more beneficial to the cassava and your pocket.

Overall, intercropping should not affect your cassava crop adversely, if you follow the instructions and do it right. Intercropping does have the potential to provide an income that could cover most, if not all your initial investments. But you have to do it right.

At the bottom of page 123, there is a photo of cassava field intercropped with corn. From the looks of it, both the cassava and corn seem to be struggling, even though, the cassava seems to be doing better than the corn. However, you will not know how well the cassava is actually doing until you harvest. That is where the *'proof of the pudding'* is. Actually, the field looks very crowded. This what we do not want, an overcrowded field. Why? Because at some time the corn will have to be harvested, and from what I see, the cassava will surely be disturbed or damaged. This not what we want.

The saying is, "One photo says a thousand words." From the looks of things, it is easy to conclude that both cassava and corn were planted randomly without any order. This is what you will have to avoid.

Let us take a look at the two illustrations on page 124. The illustration at the top left shows cassava cuttings planted in rows with corn seeds inserted in the middle of 4 (four) cuttings. See the arrow pointed at the 4 cassava cuttings forming an "X" with corn seeds planted at its intersection. This is the how you should place the seeds or seedlings when you are intercropping with short-term crops like corn, peppers, watermelon. If you do it like this, it will give each plant room to grow and limit the pressure on the cassava plant.

---

60 *As recommended by CATAS. Even though Rubber might be great to intercrop with cassava, the people at CATAS do not recommend it. Why? Because of the of the possibility of cassava diseases being transferred to the rubber trees.*

The illustration shows you how the corn is supposed to grow with the cassava when it is planted this way.

Both illustrations show order. This is the way you should intercrop your cassava field. From these illustrations one can predict how well the corn and the cassava will grow together. This is what we want. This does not only reduces competition, but it also provides order. This will allow the corn to be harvested without much interference with the cassava plants. This is what you want and should try your best to do. But you will only get this with perseverance, patience and hard work.

Of course if you are intercropping with a long-term crops like Cocoa and Oil Palm, the configurations will be different and based on the required plant spacing for the Oil Palm or Cocoa.

Take a close look at the photo below. It is a cassava field intercropped with pumpkin. See how the pumpkin has matured and is ready to be harvested before the cassava is fully grown and has established its canopy. This is ideal because the pumpkin can be harvested without damaging the cassava.

Cassava intercropped with Pumpkin.
(Photo, courtesy of CATAS)

CASSAVA HARVESTING

The first thing that you need to know or be reminded of when it comes to harvesting cassava is that it takes 9-12 (nine to twelve) months for most cassava varieties to mature, as was said earlier. I know that there might be some varieties which could be harvested in 3-6 (three to six) months. However, most cassava varieties will be fully matured in this 9-12-month period. I do know that in Grand Bassa County (Liberia), people like to prepare their Dumboy, a local delicacy, from young cassava tubers. So, they do harvest early for that purpose, but in most cases, they do not harvest the entire field.

Cassava being harvested manually can be labor-intensive.

In the ***Liberia Cassava Feasibility Study,*** several of the local varieties are listed with their harvesting times. What I would suggest is that you get adequate information on the harvesting time for the variety you would like to plant, so, that you will harvest in time. For example, the *Yellow Root* variety should be harvested at exactly 9 months after planting.

The best time to harvest cassava is during the dry season when there is less rain, but the time you harvest will really be determined by the time you plant your cassava. If you plant at the end of the rainy season, expect to start harvesting sometime between August and September. If you plant just before the beginning of the Rainy Season (February-March), expect to start harvesting in November and December. How long your harvesting process will be, will depend on the size of your farm and the yield.

Makeshift transportation.

This is what most of farmers rely on to get their produce to the market. See the challenge?

Most cassava farmers do not harvest their entire field all at once. This is due to several reasons: storage, transportation, lack of adequate roads and market access. This can be summed up as an attempt at limiting post-harvest losses (PHL). Most farmers are located long distances from the main roads and have to travel very long distances to the main market grounds. Because of the lack of transportation, many times they have to physically carry the cassava which is normally packaged in 25 kg or 50 kg bags. This means they can only transport a limited quantity at a time even if they have access to one of the local means of transportation.

Take a look at the rudimentary transporter in the photo at the bottom of the previous page. In most cases this is the only motorized transportation farmer have at their disposal. The amount of produce this vehicle can carry is limited because, not only is it human-powered, rugged and heavy, but the terrain that it must travel on is also rough, and in some cases, hilly. One can easily imagine how difficult it is for the operators. So, smart as farmers are, they harvest what they can manage to avoid spoilage (post-harvest loss); and they also know that they can lose money if there is a glut on the market (Supply and Demand).

Except you have a ready buyer, have your own processing facilities, or some means of transportation, I expect that you will have the very same experience. Remember our advice at the beginning, *"Make sure that you establish the reasons why you are getting into such a major project."*

How do you harvest and what tools do you need?

Harvesting cassava is not a real big deal. In fact, it is quite simple and only becomes a major issue when you have a very large farm, and you have larger than normal tubers, which of course is what all of us want. This is another time when the issue of labor comes into play. Because you will have to hire the manpower to get the job done. Of course, the larger the farm, the more manpower you will need.

Overall the process of harvesting cassava is quite simple; and in most cases, the tools needed are just the regular stuff (cutlass/machete, hoe and digger, and shovel), some of the same tools you would have used during land preparation and planting.

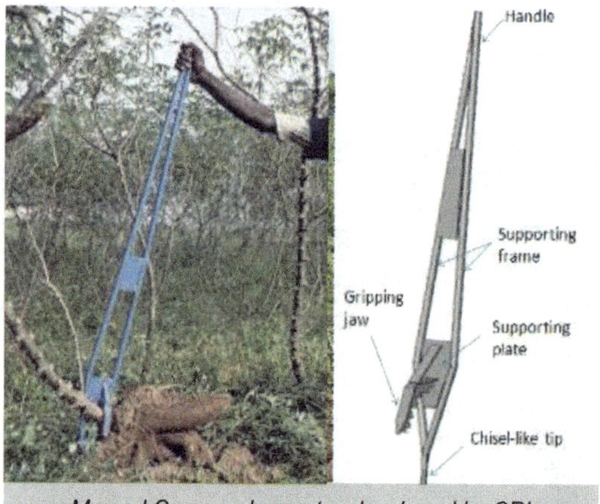

Manual Cassava harvester developed by CRI

Normally, cassava is harvested by simply digging around the roots to loosen up the soil; and then you take hold of the stalk and pull up the whole plant as seen in the photo at the top of the previous page. In most cases the tools listed above would be adequate to do the job. The photo at the top of the previous tells another story though, if you look closely. Can you tell what it is? It is taking three men to pull up the cassava. Wow! That means the roots of this cassava plant are quite large and weigh a lot. Of course this what all of us want.

However, if you do have a very large farm and have a ready buyer for the entire farm, then you should start looking at some other solutions. There are some specialized tool which have been developed by IITA, CATAS and the Crop Research Institute (CRI), of Ghana. These tools can easily be fabricated by local fabricators or welders.

If you have larger than normal tubers, special care must be taken when pulling up the plant to keep the tubers from breaking up. Fortunately, there are available some mechanical solutions. And the good thing is some of these mechanized devices are being developed and manufactured right here in Africa. There are two types of mechanical harvesters:

- Manual and
- Automated or tractor-driven.

On page 128, a manual harvester is illustrated in the photo on the left. This tool was developed by CRI.[61] As you can see, this manual type is quite simple and could easily be fabricated. The photo on the right is a fabricated manual cassava harvester developed by CATAS This harvester can also be easily fabricated.

In addition to these manual harvesters, there are several automated harvesters available. Some are standalone complete units while others have to be attached to a tractor. The two photos below show two tractor-driven cassava harvesters. The tractor-driven harvester uproots the tubers as the tractor drives though the field. Remember what we said about field preparation and planting in rows using one of the newer planting methods? Tractor-driven harvester can only work effectively if you destumped and plant orderly using one of the newer planting methods as have been recommended. The tractor-driven cassava harvester in the photo on the right was designed, developed and manufactured at Kwame Nkrumah University of Science and Technology (KNUST),[62] Kumasi, Ghana. The one on the left is one of the larger, more industrialized versions manufactured in China.

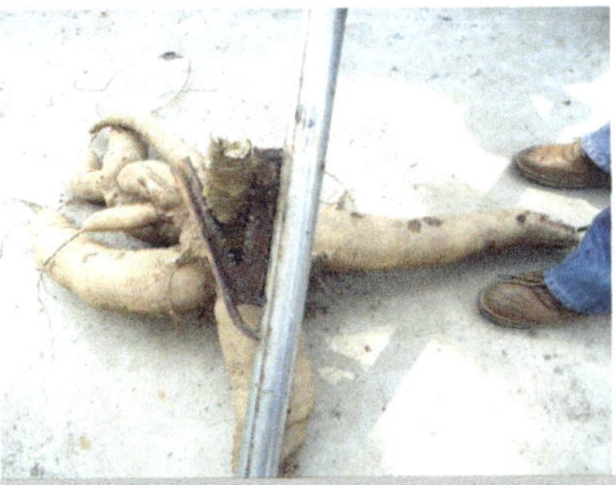

Manual Cassava harvester from CATAS

Tractor-Driven Cassava Harvesters

61. CRI, Crops Research Institute is one of the thirteen research Institutes of the Council for Scientific and Industrial Research of Ghana. CSIR-CRI evolved from the Specialists' branch of the Gold Coast Department of Agriculture.

62 KNUST– Kwame Nkrumah University of Science and Technology, established in 1952, is located in Kumasi, Ghana. KNUST is one of Africa's premiere universities for science and engineering.

The bottom line: Cost

Finances! Wow! So, not much was mentioned about finances, was it? So, we did all these calculations for seed needs and production estimates but never really talked about cost. I know that there is an inset on the cost of planting material, but those were just estimates on only one aspect of the entire process. Actually and honestly, "No!" We did not spend much time on finances, and it was intentional. The idea was to get you to read the entire guide first to get a feel of the processes involve in cassava production.

Seriously, though, knowing how much it will cost you to set up a Cassava farm or whatever crop you are considering to produce, is very important, even if it is just a personal backyard garden. You must know what you are putting into the project, especially, if you want to make some money from it.

I will revisit some of the calculations we did earlier, but before we do, I want to say something very important here. It is my recommendation that you consider creating a business plan before getting involved in any endeavour of this nature. "Business Plan!" Yes, I know it sounds scary, and it can be expensive, but a simple plan will do. Honestly, and perhaps, what is even most important is that you need to do some projections; and to do that, you need to develop a system of recordkeeping to keep track of what you are doing and what you are spending in the entire process.

As I said, this should have been one of the first things that I addressed, but I thought that it was more important to see what you were getting into first and get a feel of the kind of work that is needed to get involve in this kind of project.

Besides doing a business plan, I would also strongly recommend that you get a notebook, ledger or copybook, or anything that you can use to keep a record of all of your activities, including what you spend doing them. Write down what you are doing, have done, the amount of money you spent doing it, and the day (date) and time you did it, including, the amount of time you spent doing it. Keeping track of the entire process is, perhaps, the first management exercise you will carry out. This is not only important for your own records, but it can also provide the information you will need in the future when you do decide to do a business plan, whether you write it yourself or hire someone to do it for you.

Your records should also include the dates of what you planted, where you planted it, the quantity you planted, and the hour of the day you planted it. The information will give you the estimated time when you should be harvesting; and when to do the necessary crop maintenance chores, including fertilizer application. Please make sure that you also record when crop maintenance activities are done including when fertilizers and agrochemicals are applied with the types and quantities. This allows for traceability. Remember that word, *"traceability"*. It is very important in agricultural production and processing. Remember what we said earlier about your product or produce labels having proper information. Traceability will be discussed in more detail in my next publication, Cassava Processing, but it (traceability) simply means that if something goes wrong, you will be in a better position of being able to find the point in the process where and when it occurred, if you have the records. Remember, the new EU deforestation protocol. Traceability is an important component of it.

So the next question might be, "What should I be recording?" My suggestion is that the following information must and should be recorded:

1. Date of project start.
2. Number of workers and their salaries.
3. Classes of worker, Men, women and Youth. Why? This could be some very important data that the Ministries of Agriculture and Commerce might need. ***(Please do not hire young under-aged children!)***
4. Dates of works start and completions
5. Land purchase and cost
6. Quantity of land purchased
7. Land preparation and cost
8. Inputs purchase and cost
9. Crop planting and cost
10. Purchases with quantity and cost
11. Labour cost and the number of persons involved
12. Feeding cost
13. Transportation cost
14. Losses – parts of inputs (seed, fertilizer, chemical) which you could not use due to spoilage, wastage or theft.

This list might seem long to you, but the number of activities that you could record, and track could be a lot more. The idea here is not to bog you down with a lot of extra paper work, but it is must that you understand the importance of keeping a record of what you do, and how much you are spending doing the things that you do. Most importantly, you need to keep the receipts of items you purchase and services you pay for. Even if the person does not have a receipt to give you, try and have a receipt or payment book with you at all times. This will allow you to record the purchases you make when the vendor does not have receipts. Please do not hype up what you spend.

I can guarantee you that even I do not do it all the time, but it has its consequences, if it is not done. Because you will not only lose track of what you are spending, but at the end of the day, you will not have any idea of what the project actually cost. And in the end, you would not know when you planted what and when you should be harvesting it.

Record-keeping takes the guess-work out, and it puts you in charge. It also helps you to manage the people who work for you. Not only should you be recording the information, but make sure you store the information in a safe place where you can have easy access to it when you need it. You will not appreciate this advice until you start turning your office upside down looking for some important document or receipt.

Another thing I would suggest is that you register your business so that it becomes a legal entity. This so important if you want to open a bank account and apply for grants from the government or some donor-sponsored project. The good part of this, is that it not expensive. In Liberia, the Liberia Business Registry, in Monrovia of your county, is the place to go.

Labour Cost

This brings us to the issue of labour cost and cost in general. Yeah! Money must be spent in every step of the process, from acquiring the land (if you don't have your own), preparing the land, getting planting material, planting and finally harvesting, packaging and transporting the harvested-produce to a factory or market. The cost of labour varies from county to county, community to community and country to country. The cost of labour in Sierra Leone, Nigeria or the Ivory Coast will not be the same in Liberia; and I am sure it is not the same in all of the 36 states of Nigeria or all of the regions in Ghana, or the Gambia either.

You just have to be very careful, pay attention and be involved in the various processes because you can lose a lot of money dealing with workers and their demands. The local people and farmers will be able to help, and they might be the best people to guide you.

In Liberia, normally it will cost you from $300-$500 (three hundred to five hundred Liberian dollars) per-man-per day. This is an estimate based on previous trends. It could be more depending where you are located. In addition, you must provide feeding. Yes! You have got to provide *food* for your workers in the field. Our farmers go through the same process. Providing food for your workers is not anything new or strange, and neither is it a bad thing to do. That is just how life is in the farming business in our part of the world.

To cut down on labour cost and time, most of our farming communities use what is referred to as the "Kou System". This is a system of *shared-labour*, in which the farmers, in a particular community or district, come together as a group and work together to clear and prepare each other's farms. The system is also used at harvest. Basically, farmers go from farm to farm providing labour and expertise to their fellow farmers with the expectation that they will receive the same courtesy when it is time to prepare their individual farms. The farmer in whose farm they are working in at a particular time is responsible to provide the food. In some cases, he or she provides libations.

If your farm is located in a major farming community, the Kou system could be employed based on the arrangements you and the farmers agreed on. Of course, this will greatly depend on the relationship you have developed with the community and their leaders. Perhaps, you might be able to save some money. Remember you have to feed the workers, and perhaps provide some minimum compensation; and remember, some libations.

LEAD FARMER STRATEGY

The Lead Farmer is another strategy that one could use to help solve labour issues, including cost. However, the Lead Farmer strategy was not originally meant for these purposes. It was meant to be used as a training tool where a group of farmers could be trained in agricultural practices and at the same time be provided extension and advisory services under the lead and supervision of an identified *Lead Farmer* from within the community. This is one of the methodology used in one of the MOA IFAD[63] sponsored projects in Liberia, the Agriculture Smallholder Rehabilitation Support Project (ASRP), in which I served as an Agribusiness Consultant. I think that you could use this strategy also.

How does this work? In the Lead Farmer strategy, a well known model farmer with at least one hectare of farmland is identified by the community. This farmer is recruited and selected to lead another 19 farmers, who are also recruited from within the community or from adjacent towns and villages. Together the 20 (twenty) farmers, including the lead farmer, who serves as a supervisor and point of contact, are provided inputs and agronomic training. The major objective of this model is that the 19 farmers working along with the lead farmer, will take what they have learned and incorporate it in their own farming practices, and hopefully become productive farmers themselves.

For the managers of the project, they not only save money and resources by bringing all 20 farmers together in one place, but they are also able to provide training and resources to a lot more farmers than they would have been able to do, normally. However, as good and effective as this model is, there are drawbacks.

One of the main drawbacks is a feeling amongst the other farmers that the *lead farmer* is favoured and getting compensated, and they are not. The other is that this model, in this particular project, focussed more on production and not processing. In my opinion, for the "Lead Farmer" model to really work, both production and processing must be included in the training.

You can use this model, but you will have play the role of the lead farmer and use your farm or project as a training facility for a number of farmers from the community

[63] *IFAD: International Fund for Agricultural Development is a UN agency base in Rome (Italy). It funds agriculture and development projects.*

or beyond. These farmers could serve a dual purpose - both as workers and trainees; and eventually, they could become out-growers who could provide you with additional produce to meet your production needs in the future.

How would this work? Instead of hiring ordinary farm workers, recruit farmers and offer them both a job with pay and an opportunity for training. You will have to spell this out in the beginning. Then provide them training and capacity-building in various agronomic practices which would make them better farmers and an asset to you. Additionally, you could provide them with inputs like improved seeds and tools to use on their own farms. You could enter into and agreement or MOU with them on a scheme that would allow them to pay a minimum for the inputs and with an agreement to sell what they, eventually, grow on their farms to you.

This could not only provide you with a dependable workforce, but a workforce that you can trust, and that has an attachment to you. your project or business; and at the same time provide an additional source of raw material for your project. If you do this right using your own insights and innovation, your workers might look at themselves as partners to you rather than just workers. This could end up saving you more than money on labour. I would suggest that you do this, that you get the local leadership (chiefs) involved.

This could very well protect you in the future if the farmers do not live up to their part of the agreement, or if you have problems meeting your obligations. Remember, nothing is perfect. There are always possibilities for trouble, in spite of good intentions. Consulting the local leadership and getting them involved in the beginning will go a long way in resolving issues when they occurred, whether you or your workers are at fault. Do not ignore the local leaders, then come to them when you encounter problems.

Epilogue: Making sense out of it all

There is so much talk about Cassava and agriculture in general with the accompanying slogans, jargons and all the declarations and promises. So, what is one to make out of all this palaver (noise) about agriculture solving all of our problems, rescuing our economies and enriching our people and improving the quality of their lives? I do not know about you, but sometimes, I wonder if the people who are doing all this talking and making these declarations, especially the politicians, really know what they are talking about; or if they are really serious about transforming our countries' economies and the peoples' wellbeing through agriculture? I always hear them talk about the "value chain" and "value addition" approach.

I do not want to sound like a *"Mister Know It All"*, but somehow I am not really convinced that many of these politicians or academics really know what they are talking about; or whether they have the solutions or even comprehend the work it entails, or the challenges our farmers go through daily. Honestly and seriously, I really do not want to second guess anyone, but I am just a bit concerned.

The truth is that agriculture is the way. The AU has demonstrated this and shown its commitment through the creation of the Comprehensive Africa Agriculture Development Programme (CAADP) in 2003, some 20 (twenty) years ago at Maputo (Mozambique). In 2014, at Malabo, Equatorial Guinea, the African Heads of State and governments (HSOG), our leaders, including our own president, once again, recommitted to the CAADP through the Malabo Declarations with its Seven Commitments. Now, the AU has created the African Continental Free Trade Area (AfCFTA), the largest free trade area in the world, which offers us so many opportunities to improve our nations' economy and the lives of all of our peoples in our individual countries and across Africa.

And as I was in the final stages of editing the "Guide" for publication, the AU was conducting a series of consultations with African agricultural stakeholders, large and small, women and men, youth and the physically challenged across Africa, in every region and economic block to shape the next generation of the CAADP: *the post Malabo Agenda.* These consultations had been on going since March 2024 and will culminate in January 2025 at Kampala, Uganda, as the Kampala Declaration (2026-2036), a pivotal instrument of Agenda 2063: The Africa we want. The question is. "Are we ready?" And the next is, "Are we serious?"

In fact, this CAADP (AU) declaration to use agriculture as the foundation for economic development is not new. Our (Liberia) first president, Joseph Jenkins Roberts, made the same declaration 176 years ago on July 26, 1848[64] during his Inaugural Address - declaring that agriculture would be the bedrock of our (Liberia) economic de-

[64] *See President Joseph Jenkins Roberts Inaugural Address, July 26, 1848.*

velopment. Did it work then? Yes it did, for some time, until outside intervention and maleficence by the colonial powers of the day, to thwart our economy and hence destroyed our nation. Perhaps, it was an attempt to absorb our nation, the only independent African country (at that time) into their colonial sphere. I am not going into any history here because this is not what this publication is about. The information is available if you want it.[65] Just do the research. Our research institute, CARI, established in 1955, is one of the oldest research institutions in Africa, and, perhaps, the only one that was not created by a colonizing power. We built it!

Now, some 176 years later, another president is proclaiming Agriculture as the primary instrument in his government's development agenda, the ARREST Agenda for Inclusive Development (AAID).[66] Is it going to be any different from past declarations? I realize that we (Liberia) have a new National Agriculture Development Plan (NADP), but we have had others, LASIP (I & II), PRS. Did these programs have any significant impact? The recently announced agriculture budget is, dismally, below the 10% than what we, along with other African states of the African Union (AU), committed to at Maputo and Malabo. In fact, we are 4 points below the average (5%)[68] of ECOWAS member states.

With such a low agriculture budget, can there be any significant transformation considering the challenges our farmers face? Some might argue that, perhaps, the various donor-funded agricultural projects, somehow, will fill in the gap in direct budgetary support to the sector. Even if this argument is true and valid. There is no evidence from the last four CAADP Biennial Review reports thar support this. Not only does the government have to live up to these commitments, but it also has the responsibility to take the lead in investing in the necessary infrastructures that will fuel the growth and transformation of the sector that is desired by both the ARREST agenda and the AU's CAADP.

Cassava is not only our second staple, but it is one of many crops that can contribute, significantly, to economic development, wealth creation and change the lives of our people, especially, our famers (men, women, the youth and the physically challenged). However, simply growing and processing cassava or any crop, for that matter, will not achieve anything significant, if we and our leaders do not work together to create the enabling environment and build the necessary infrastructure (access to finance, electricity, running water and irrigation systems, markets, roads, storage facilities, Agriculture Extension and Advisory services, etc.) that makes up the agriculture value chain and which are needed and necessary to enable the agriculture sector to actually work.

---

[66] *Multinational Investment and The Development of an Export Industry: Rubber in LIBERIA, Anismesh Ghosal*

[67] *The ARREST Agenda for Inclusive Development (AAID), which includes the Public Sector Investment Plan (PSIP) and the fifteen County Development Agendas (CDAs), is the official development policy of Liberian President Joseph Nyuma Boakai.*

[68] *A Review of Agriculture Sector Performance in West Africa (ECOWAS Regional Join Sector Review 2020)*

Through out this guide, I have mentioned some mechanized solution, including combine harvesters, which are mainly used in the grain industry. I have mentioned this because if we really want to revolutionized agricultural production in Liberia and Africa in general, we need to mechanized. Not just purchasing equipment from abroad for use here, but perhaps, to even fabricate and manufacture some of these machines here in Africa, and perhaps, even in Liberia. Additionally, even if we have to purchase these equipment, Liberian entrepreneurs must be given the opportunity to participate in the procurement processes. However, mechanization alone will not solve all of the problems associated with agriculture production. We need an innovative-integrated agriculture production system (value chain) that will include irrigation solutions, which we have mentioned above. And serious attention must be placed on resolving the issues of post-harvest losses and creating and equitable functional market system and the transportation infrastructure to support it.

In addition to all that have been mentioned above, agriculture must be sold to the people and would-be entrepreneurs as a viable endeavour. The agricultural Value Chain is vast, and there are lots of opportunities within it which need to be unlocked and harnessed. These opportunities must be privatized, private-sector driven and sold to the people, particularly, Liberian and African investors and entrepreneurs; and the appropriate environment and protections created, so that people's investments will not go down the drain. The government must consider public private partnerships (PPP) interventions, as prescribe by the CAADP, that involve both Liberian and foreign entrepreneurs with some preferences given to Liberian-owned businesses not just Liberian-registered businesses. These are two distinct entities.

In addition, I believe that there is a need to diversify our diet and our production system. While rice and cassava are very important, and their productions systems must be developed and improved upon, we have other crops and plants that we need to develop and promote. I really do not think cassava, rice, cocoa, coffee and rubber alone, will lift our people out of poverty. There is a need to look at other crops, especially those with export potential.

The truth is that Liberian farmers and African farmers, in general, are working hard in some difficult circumstances, and they are making efforts and, actually, are the backbone of the African economy, in spite of the many challenges we listed above plus the added pressure to mitigate the global climate and environmental crisis. The groups of photos on pages 140 and 141 are illustrations of some of the fruits of their labour and the opportunities they present. They also showcase the many challenges that Liberian and African farmers face. I call these illustrations a *Pictorial SWOT Analysis.*

This Guide is just one instrument which I hope can help the process. I have done much to make it a global endeavour, even though, my primary target audience has always been Liberians. I hope I was able to achieve some degree of the globalization. There is so much more to learn and do. I do hope you find it useful.

A Pictorial SWOT Analysis

A group of pictures speak a thousand words! — Strengths, Weaknesses, Opportunities & Threats in pictures!

Challenges: 12 stories of Strengths, Weaknesses Opportunities, and Treats

1. Makeshift bridge somewhere in Nimba County - Weakness; 2. Bad Roads (Threat & Weakness - PHL); 3. Transporting Plantain Decent road, but with people sitting on produce– PHL (Strength, Weakness & Opportunity) 4. Primitive Cassava Press (Weakness & Opportunity); 5. Plantain at Red Light Market - Market Access but poor storage facility– PHL. (Opportunity, Weakness & Threat); 6. Fruits availability, Red Light Market

(All photos taken by author.)

A Pictorial SWOT Analysis

A group of pictures speak a thousand words– Strengths, Weaknesses, Opportunities & Threats in pictures!

Challenges: Stories of Strengths, Weaknesses Opportunities, and Treats

1. Fine tomatoes grown by Liberian farmer (Opportunity & Strength); 2. Fruits availability, Red Light Market (Opportunity); 3. Kola nuts in Foya Market (Lofa County), Opportunity;; 5. Cocoa Drying in Lofa County – Strength, Weakness, Opportunity; 5. Cassava Production (Strength, Opportunity); and 6. Fufu Market at Market, Bokay's Town (Grand Bassa County) - Opportunity, lack of storage is a Threat.

(All photos taken by author except 5, courtesy of NCSCC)

Good luck!

See you at harvest and hope you have a great harvest.

APPENDIX

APPENDIX 1: ACRONYMS

ACP, African Caribbean Pacific
AfCFTA, Africa Continental Free Trade Area (Agreement)
ARREST, Agriculture, Roads, Rule of Law, Education, Sanitation and Tourism
AU, African Union
CAADP, Comprehensive Africa Agriculture Development Programme
CAGR, Compound Annual Growth Rate
CARI:, Central Agriculture Research Institute
CATAS, Chinese Academy of Tropical Agriculture
CMD, Cassava Mosaic Disease
EC, European Commission
ECOWAS, Economic Community of West African Countries
EPA, Environment Protection Agency
EU, European Union
FAO, Food and Agriculture ORGANIATION
FBI, Fortune Business Insights
HQCF, High Quality Cassava Flour
ITC, International Trade Center
IFAD, International Fund for Agricultural Development
IITA, International Institute for Tropical Agriculture
INMARC, International Market Analysis Research and Consulting
LASIP, Liberian Agriculture Sector Investment Programme
LLA, Liberian Land Authority
LRA, Land Reform Act
MOA, Ministry of Agriculture (Liberia)
MOCI, Ministry of Commerce and Industry
NADP, National Agriculture Development Program
NEPAD, New Partnership for African Development
NCSCC, National Cassava Sector Coordinating Committee
NRDC, National Resource Defense Council
PHL, Post-Harvest Loss
PNAS, Proceedings of The National Academy of Sciences
SRI, System of Rice Intensification
SWOT, Strength Weakness Opportunity Threats
WB, World Bank
WEF, World Economic Forum

APPENDIX 2: REGIONAL ECONOMIC COMMUNITIES (RECS) OF AFRICA

1. Arab Maghreb Union (UMA)
2. Common Market for Eastern and Southern Africa (COMESA)
3. Community of Sahel-Saharan States (CEN-SAD)
4. East African Community (EAC)
5. Economic Community of Central African States (ECCAS)
6. Economic Community of West African States (ECOWAS)
7. Intergovernmental Authority on Development (IGAD)
8. Southern African Development Community (SADC)

Appendix 3: Important Agricultural Resource Institutions

Central Agriculture Research Institute
Monrovia-Gbarnga Highway
Suakoko, Bong County, Liberia
Contact: Mercy Kou Lah
Email: lah.mercy@yahoo.com
Phone: +231 776 445745

Program Management Unit (PMU)
Ministry of Agriculture
Old LIPSUCO Building
Somalia Drive (Gardnersville)
Paynesville, Liberia

Liberia Standards Authority (LISA)
Ministry of Public Works Compound
Lynch Street
Monrovia Liberia
Contact: +231880918823
info@lisa.gov.lr

National Cassava Sector Coordinating Committee
Contact: Joseph J/ Morris
Phone: +231 (886)923682/+231 (777)634256
Email: info@ncsccl.org

International Institute of Tropical Agriculture (IITA)
Headquarters:
PMB 5320, Oyo Road, Ibadan 200001
Oyo State, Nigeria
Tel: +234 700800IITA
Email: iita@cgiar.org

Chinese Academy of Tropical Agriculture Sciences (CATAS)
4 Xueyuan Rd, Longhua District, Haikou
Haikou, Hainan, China, 571101
Web site: http://www.catas.cn
Email: catasgjhzc@126.com
Phone number (s): +86-898-66962983

Liberian Land Authority
Ashmun and Gurley Streets
Monrovia, Liberia

Soil Labs
University of Liberia
Fendell Campus
Fendell, Montserrado County

Environmental Protection Agency (EPA)
EPA Laboratory
EPA Offices (Ground Floor)
Tubman Boulevard
Sinkor, Monrovia, Liberia
Contact:
Rafael Sarji Ngumbu, Manager
Email: rngumbu@epa.gov.lr

Liberia Business Registry
Asmun and Nelson Streets
Monrovia, Liberia
http://www.lbr.gov.lr; info@lbr.gov.lr.

Community of Hope Agriculture Project (CHAP)
Zubah Town, Paynesville
Liberia
Contact:
Robert Bimba
National Project Coordinator
RICOWAS Project
National Facilitator for SRI/CRRP Liberia
WhatsApp: +231-770-155-844
Email: robertbimba@yahoo.com/robertb@chapliberia.org
Website: www.chapliberia.org

Women in Agriculture for Sustainable Development (WASUDEV)
GSA Road-Kissi Camp Junction
Paynesville, Liberia
Contact:
Hawa Dunor-Varney
+231 770110772
Email: womeninagriculture4dev@gmail.com

Appendix 4: Cassava varieties catalogued by CARI

The table below is a listing of Cassava varieties courtesy of the Roots and Tuber Division of CARII's Crops Department.

No	List of cassava variety	Type of cassava	Type of varieties	Mature period	Yield /ha	Irrigated filed
1	Bassa Girl	Local	Poundable/ Sweet cassava	6-9 months	5-9 tons/ha	Planting is done through-out the year
2	Martardi	Local	Poundable/ Sweet cassava	6-9 months	5-9 tons/ha	Planting is done through-out the year
3	Butter cassava	Local	Poundable/ Sweet cassava	6-9 months	5-9 tons/ha	Planting is done through-out the year
4	Ghana Girl	Local	Poundable/ Sweet cassava	6-9 months	5-9 tons/ha	Planting is done throughout the year
6	Bentelay	Local	Poundable/ Sweet cassava	6-9 months	10-15 tons/ha	Planting is done through-out the year
7	Mana Gbolu	Local	Poundable/ Sweet cassava	6-9 months	10-15 tons/ha	Planting is done through-out the year
8	CARICASS-2	Improved	Industrial / Bitter cassava	6-9 months	40 tons/ha	Planting is done through-out the year
9	92/0057	Improved	Industrial / Bitter cassava	6-9 months	40 tons/ha	Planting is done through-out the year
10	SC -6068	Improved	Poundable/ Sweet cassava	6-9 months	40 tons/ha	Planting is done through-out the year
11	01/1206- yellow root cassava	Improved	Industrial / Bitter cassava	6-9 months	40 tons/ha	Planting is done through-out the year
12	01/1235- yellow root cassava	Improved	Industrial / Bitter cassava	6-9 months	25-38 tons/ha	Planting is done through-out the year
13	95/0289	Improved	Industrial / Bitter cassava	6-9 months	25-38 tons/ha	Planting is done through-out the year
14	01/0040	Improved	Industrial / Bitter cassava	6-9 months	50 tons/ha	Planting is done through-out the year
15	95/0303 yellow root cassava	Improved	Industrial / Bitter cassava	6-9 months	40 tons/ha	Planting is done through-out the year
16	95/0166	Improved	Industrial / Bitter cassava	6-9 months	25-38 tons/ha	Planting is done through-out the year
17	95/0416	Improved	Industrial / Bitter cassava	6-9 months	25-38 tons/ha	Planting is done through-out the year
18	00/0357	Improved	Industrial / Bitter cassava	6-9 months	25-38 tons/ha	Planting is done through-out the year
19	MH 95/0414	Improved	Industrial / Bitter cassava	6-9 months	25-38 tons/ha	Planting is done through-out the year

Update Cassava variety table continued

No	List of cassava variety	Type of cassava	Type of varieties	Mature period	Yield /ha	Irrigated filed
20	91/0430	Improved	Industrial / Bitter cassava	6-9 months	25-38 tons/ha	Planting is done throughout the year
21	92/0097	Improved	Industrial / Bitter cassava	6-9 months	25-38 tons/ha	Planting is done throughout the year
22	01/1371	Improved	Industrial / Bitter cassava	6-9 months	42 tons/ha	Planting is done throughout the year
23	98/0289	Improved	Industrial / Bitter cassava	6-9 months	50 tons/ha	Planting is done throughout the year
24	CARICASS I	Improved	Industrial / Bitter cassava	6-9 months	25-38 tons/ha	Planting is done throughout the year
25	CARICASS II	Improved	Industrial / Bitter cassava	6-9 months	25-38 tons/ha	Planting is done throughout the year
26	CARICASS III	Improved	Industrial / Bitter cassava	6-9 months	25-38 ton/ha	Planting is done throughout the year
27	98/0505	Improved	Industrial / Bitter cassava	6-9 months	40 ton/ha	Planting is done throughout the year
28	01/1412	Improved	Industrial / Bitter cassava	6-9 months	25-38 ton/ha	Planting is done throughout the year
29	95/0166	Improved	Industrial / Bitter cassava	6-9 months	40 ton/ha	Planting is done throughout the year
30	01/1371 yellow root cassava	Improved	Industrial / Bitter cassava	6-9 months	40 ton/ha	Planting is done throughout the year
31	TME-419	Improved	Industrial / Bitter cassava	6-9 months	40 ton/ha	Planting is done throughout the year

Appendix 5: Publications

Publication 1: Liberia National Cassava Strategy

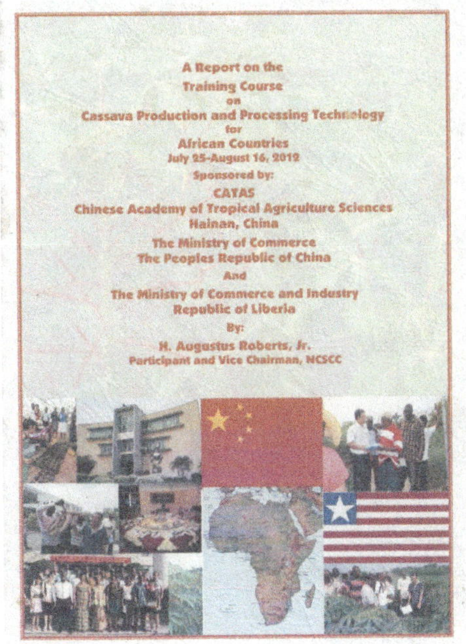

NOTES

Made in the USA
Las Vegas, NV
07 April 2025

20630529R00085